VOYAGE WITH THE LABRADOR ESKIMOS 1880–1881

Johan Adrian Jacobsen

VOYAGE WITH THE LABRADOR ESKIMOS 1880–1881

Translation of Jacobsen's diary (1879-10 to 1880-06-27, 1881-02-21 to 1881-06-25), Jacobsen's correspondence, excerpt from *Ein Seemansleben*, and the ship registration documents.   Dieter Riedel

Translation of Jacobsen's diary (1880-06-28 to 1881-01-20) and excerpt from *Eventyrlige Farter*.   Hartmut Lutz

Project editor, coordinator and layout designer   France Rivet

Cover page: Illustration by M. Hoffmann, published in *Beiträge über leben und treiben der Eskimos in Labrador und Grönland*. Berlin, 1880. Colouring by Diane Mongeau.

Cataloguing data available from Library and Archives Canada.

© Hartmut Lutz, Dieter Riedel and Polar Horizons

All rights reserved. The use of any part of this publication reproduced, transmitted in any form or by any means, electronic, mechanical, photocopying, recording, or otherwise, or stored in a retrieval system, without prior written consent of the publisher, is an infringement of copyright law.

Legal Deposit, 2019
Bibliothèque et Archives nationales du Québec
Library and Archives Canada

Second edition
ISBN 978-1-7750815-3-1 (paperback), 978-1-7750815-4-8 (epub)

Polar Horizons Inc.
27 De Cotignac Street
Gatineau, Quebec J8T 8E4
info@polarhorizons.com / www.polarhorizons.com/en

To the memory of

Abraham
Maria
Nuggasak
Paingu
Sara
Tigianniak
Tobias
Ulrike
and
Johan Adrian Jacobsen

To all Nunatsiavummiut and
to the descendants of the Jacobsen family.

Table of Contents

List of Illustrations 11
Foreword 15
Introduction 19
Translators' Preliminary Remarks 45
Acknowledgments 47

Johan Adrian Jacobsen's Diary 49
   Voyage to Norway to Buy a Ship 51
   Sailing the New Ship to Hamburg 55
   In Hamburg for Outfitting 57
   Sailing to Greenland on the *Eisbär* 61
   Recruiting in Jakobshavn 87
   Departure from Jakobshavn 95
   Voyage to Cumberland Sound 97
   Voyage in Davis Strait 103
   Arrival in Labrador 107
   In Nachvak 121
   From Labrador to Europe 131
   Storm Near Heligoland 141
   On the Elbe and Arrival at Hamburg 145
   Stay in Hamburg and in Berlin 149
   Stay in Prague and in Frankfurt 153
   Stay in Darmstadt 157
   Stay in Crefeld 159
   Stay and Death in Paris 165

After the Inuit's Death 179

Excerpts From Johan Adrian Jacobsen's Other Publications 197

Excerpt from *Eventyrlige Farter, Fortalte for Ungdommen* 199
Excerpt From *Ein Seemansleben* 205

Johan Adrian Jacobsen's Correspondence 209

1880-07-07 — 1st Letter to the North Greenland Inspector 211
1880-07-14 — North Greenland Inspector's Reply 212
1880-07-20 — 2nd Letter to the North Greenland Inspector ... 214
1880-11-09 — Letter from Carl Hagenbeck 216
1880-11-12 — Letter from Carl Hagenbeck 217
1880-11-13 — Letter from Edgar Bauer 218
1880-12-26 — Letter from Carl Hagenbeck 219
1881-01-10 — Letter from Henriette Kühne 220
1881-01-13 — Letter from Henriette Kühne 222
1881-01-14 — List of Artifacts / Invoice for Prof. Bogišić 224
1881-01-14 — Letter from Carl Friedrich Ludwig Kühne 226
1881-01-16 — Letter from Carl Hagenbeck 228
1881-01-17 — Letter from J. M. Jacobsen and Henriette Kühne 229
1881-01-20 — Letters from Edgar Bauer and Adolf Bastian 234
1881-01-23 — Letter from Adolf Schoepf 236
1881-01-24 — Letter from Adolf Schoepf 238
1881-01-27 — Letter from Carl Hagenbeck 240
1881-01-27 — Letter from Henriette Kühne and J. M. Jacobsen 241
1881-01-27 — Letter from Adolf Schoepf 243
1881-01-30 — Letter from Albertina Lutz 245
1881-02-05 — Letter from Edgar Bauer 247
1881-02-07 — Letter from Carl Friedrich Ludwig Kühne 249
1881 - Letter from Henriette Kühne 251
1881-02-15 — Postcard from Adolf Schoepf 253
1881-02-17 — Letter from Carl Hagenbeck 254

1881-02-17 — Letter from Adolf Schoepf 255
1881-03-27 — Letter from Edgar Bauer.. 256
1881-04-04 — Letter from Adolf Bastian 258
1881-04-05 — Letter from Adolf Bastian.......................................259
1881-09-23 — Letter from Carl Hagenbeck 260
1881-12-02 — Letter from Carl Hagenbeck................................ 262

The *Eisbär* 265
    Ship's Registration Documents 267

Afterword 277

Archival Sources 283

Other References 289

Index of People and Place Names 293

List of Illustrations

Fig. 1 Johan Adrian Jacobsen. 1881. _____13
Fig. 2 Landing in Hebron, Labrador. _____20
Fig. 3 Hans Blohm and France Rivet. _____22
Fig. 4 France Rivet, Hartmut Lutz, and Jacqueline Thun. _____26
Fig. 5 Hartmut Lutz and France Rivet. _____27
Fig. 6 Johannes Lampe and Hartmut Lutz. _____28
Fig. 7 Hartmut Lutz reading a letter from Carl Hagenbeck. _____29
Fig. 8 January 3, 1881, prescription by Dr. Panneval. _____30
Fig. 9 Dieter Riedel translating Jacobsen's correspondence. _____31
Fig. 10 Page 1 of the registration documents for the Eisbär. _____32
Fig. 11 Signatures on ship registration documents. _____33
Fig. 12 Cathrine Baglo searching custom records. _____35
Fig. 13 Portraits of J. A. Jacobsen and his wife. _____38
Fig. 14 Johannes Lampe, Adrian Jacobsen, and Kerstin Bedranowsky. 40
Fig. 15 Jacobsen Family house on Risøya, Norway. _____41
Fig. 16 Kenth Thomas Mikalsen welcoming us on Risøya. _____42
Fig. 17 Portraits - Nansen, Amundsen, Jacobsen, and Sverdrup. Risøya. 42
Fig. 18 Kirsten K. Barton Holiman and Hartmut Lutz. Risøya. _____43
Fig. 19 View from the kitchen window. Risøya. _____43
Fig. 20 Hamburg Harbour, 1883. _____59
Fig. 21 Map of Jacobsen's 1880 travels in Greenland and Labrador. _____60
Fig. 22 Celebration on the Eisbär. _____88
Fig. 23 Zion church and doctor's house. Jakobshavn. ca 1900. _____90
Fig. 24 Kujanje, Kokkik, Okabak, Maggak, Ane, and Regine. _____92
Fig. 25 Iceberg, Labrador coast. _____105
Fig. 26 Hebron from the hills. _____107
Fig. 27 Eskimo grave in Labrador. _____109

Fig. 28 Collecting in Hebron graves. _____ 111
Fig. 29 Ford's House - Last house and the North Atlantic Coast. ____ 123
Fig. 30 Ford's House. Nachvak Bay, Northern Labrador. _____ 123
Fig. 31 The family recruited in Nachvak. October 1880. _____ 126
Fig. 32 The family from Hebron. October 1880. _____ 129
Fig. 33 Iceberg along the Labrador coast near Nachvak Fjord. _____ 132
Fig. 34 Tigianniak calming a storm. _____ 141
Fig. 35 Heligoland, ca 1890-1900. _____ 143
Fig. 36 Map of Jacobsen's 1880 travels in Europe. _____ 144
Fig. 37 Tigianniak smoking pipe in his tent. _____ 150
Fig. 38 Tobias, Paingu, Tigianniak, Ulrike, and Sara. _____ 151
Fig. 39 Abraham and Tobias demonstrating a seal hunt. _____ 154
Fig. 40 Tigianniak, Nuggasak, and Paingu inside their hut. _____ 155
Fig. 41 Nuggasak. _____ 158
Fig. 42 Concert hall and restaurant at the Bockum zoo (near Crefeld). 160
Fig. 43 Tigianniak, Paingu, and Nuggasak. _____ 162
Fig. 44 Alexianer Hospital, Crefeld, 1883. _____ 163
Fig. 45 Train station in Aachen. _____ 165
Fig. 46 Ulrike and Maria. _____ 168
Fig. 47 Tigianniak. _____ 169
Fig. 48 Hopital St-Louis, Paris. Bichat Street entrance. _____ 170
Fig. 49 Abraham. _____ 174
Fig. 50 Carl Hagenbeck around 1890. _____ 178
Fig. 51 The Tower of London from the Thames, 1886. _____ 181
Fig. 52 Shipping Wild Animals in the London Docks. _____ 182
Fig. 53 Reiherstieg shipyard, Hamburg, 1840. _____ 184
Fig. 54 Head of Nachvak Lake. _____ 200

Fig. 1 Johan Adrian Jacobsen. 1881.
(Collection of Anne Kirsti Jacobsen)

Foreword

By Cathrine Baglo
Tromsø Museum — Universitetsmuseet
October 2018

As a scholar at Tromsø University Museum in Northern Norway, researching the live ethnographic exhibitions of Sámi and the part Johan Adrian Jacobsen played as Carl Hagenbeck's agent, I became acquainted with the heart-wrenching story of the Labrador Inuit in Europe more than fifteen years ago. Since then layers of this story have been revealed, not least through the scrutinizing efforts of France Rivet.

At the outset of my PhD dissertation, it seemed self-evident to understand the live ethnographic exhibitions and the activities of Jacobsen and Hagenbeck as mere acts of the Western world's denigration and exploitation of indigenous peoples. However, dealing with the research material – contemporary newspapers, photographs, contracts, personal accounts and histories kept alive within Sámi societies, and not least, Jacobsen's diaries and extensive archival documents – I realized that they were much more, and that this interpretation, paradoxical as it might seem, often came at the cost of the integrity of the people involved.

The majority of the Sámi presenters I identified – almost 400 – embarked voluntarily on the exhibitions. Most of them welcomed the opportunities they offered. They travelled abroad with clear intentions of communicating information about their culture to foreign audiences. They expressed pride in their traditions, experienced the world, and secured economic means necessary for their survival under colonialism. Some even participated in such exhibitions several times and certain families participated over generations. They often had exceptional experiences and their stories became legendary folklore within their own communities. Frequently they also gave rise to a particular status. Such was the case of Kujagi (Kujanje), the Inuk Jacobsen recruited in Jakobshavn in Greenland for Hagenbeck in 1877 and whose experiences in Europe were radically different from Abraham Ulrikab's. Kujagi became known as the 'Baron' in Western Greenland due to his stay in Europe and the money he earned there. Kujagi wanted to go back with Jacobsen in 1880, but the Danish colonial official imposed a ban. Kujagi perceived the year in Europe as the happiest of his life.

It was hardly a coincidence that the heyday of the ethnographic exhibitions, from approximately 1875 to 1900/1910, coincided with the palmy days of racial theory and social Darwinism. At a time when it was still unusual for researchers to make field studies, the displays doubled as laboratories for various (physical) anthropological investigations. The story of Jacobsen taking Paingu's skullcap after the autopsy and the way the Labrador Inuit's remains made it to the *Muséum national d'histoire naturelle* where five of the skeletons were mounted for display, is characteristic of the history of museum collections of the time. Yet, it is not the only story. Indigenous presenters, contemporary public, organizers, and impresarios experienced and perceived these exhibitions in a variety of ways. For some presenters the outcome was terribly tragic, for others not.

Voyage With the Labrador Eskimos, 1880–1881 testifies to the complexity and ambiguity of history. The book is based on Johan Adrian Jacobsen's account of his experiences with the Inuit he brought from Labrador for Hagenbeck in 1880. Jacobsen was a native of the island of Risøya near Tromsø. After leaving a career as captain of an Arctic hunting and sealing ship, he made a name for himself as a recruiter of indigenous peoples for Hagenbeck. His portfolio also included the collection of artifacts for museums. Jacobsen recruited both Sámi from Norway and Sweden, Inuit from Greenland, Sioux from South Dakota, Nuxalk from British Columbia, and Inuit from Labrador for Hagenbeck.

Because the live ethnographic exhibitions contributed to stereotypes that still persist, it is important to return to the historical sources to better understand the context of events, actions, and relations that have been lost over time. This will aid a fuller and more complete understanding of this exhibition practice, both from the perspective of the organizers and the indigenous presenters. *Voyage With the Labrador Eskimos, 1880–1881* does precisely that. The book is a translation of Jacobsen's diary for the period he spent with the Labrador Inuit and a complement to *In the Footsteps of Abraham Ulrikab* published by Rivet in 2014.

In this second edition, new sections have been translated, the introduction is expanded and updated with new findings. While Abraham Ulrikab's account of the Inuit's experiences in Europe has been translated and published,[1] Jacobsen's accounts of his work as an agent for Hagenbeck has never been brought to a larger reading public.

In addition, this second edition includes correspondence between Jacobsen and the Governor of Greenland, from family, friends, and museum employees; as well as documents regarding registration of the ship *Eisbär*. These documents are brought together without comment allowing the historical sources to speak for themselves. The translation of Jacobsen's diary and the added context to what may seem like details, offer new insight into the events that unfolded in Labrador and Europe, and the relations between Jacobsen, Hagenbeck, and the Inuit.

---

[1] Abraham's original diary in Inuktitut has yet to be located. It was returned to his family in Labrador following his death. A moravian missionary in Hebron translated it to German. The English translation of the German translation is published in *The Diary of Abraham Ulrikab: Text and Context* (see Lutz, Hartmut et al. 2005) and is reprinted in *In the Footsteps of Abraham Ulrikab* (see Rivet 2014).

Introduction

By France Rivet

As I sat down to write the introduction to this second edition of *Voyage with the Labrador Eskimos, 1880–1881*, I opened Johan Adrian Jacobsen's 1880 diary and looked for his August 10, 1880, entry. I wanted to see where exactly he was on that day 138 years ago.

I could not have picked a better day: at 7 p.m. on August 10, 1880, Johan Adrian Jacobsen's ship, *Eisbär*, anchored in Hebron, Labrador, a small community of about 200 souls. Fifty years earlier, in 1830, Moravian missionaries had chosen this Inuit seal hunting site, known as Kangerdluksoak, as their fourth and northernmost mission along the Labrador coast. They gave it the biblical name of Hebron.

Jacobsen immediately went ashore and met with the Moravian missionaries. Undoubtedly, several Inuit also came to greet this unexpected visitor. Abraham, husband of Ulrike, was most likely one of them.

The missionaries were appalled at Jacobsen's project to hire Inuit, bring them back to Europe and display them in front of crowds. When Jacobsen explained that the six Greenlanders who travelled to Europe with him in 1877 had returned home rich and famous, the missionaries replied that their souls must have been ruined.

Fig. 2 Landing in Hebron, Labrador.
(Photo: France Rivet, 2016)

But, for Abraham, a seed was planted. Life had been difficult. The fact that he was no longer able to properly provide for his family and widowed mother was a heavy weight on his shoulders. Could Jacobsen's offer be God's answer to his prayers to end his family's misery? The money he would earn in exchange for work that seemed relatively easy, would improve their living conditions, and allow him to pay back his own and his late father's debts at the mission store. Nevertheless, such a decision could not be taken lightly, especially as it would mean having to go against the missionaries.

Six days later, Jacobsen had still not convinced any of the Inuit to follow him to Europe. His last resort was to head to the fjords of Northern Labrador where Inuit who had not been Christianized lived.

Abraham agreed to be Jacobsen's interpreter on this trip. On August 16, 1880, the *Eisbär* weighed anchor and headed for Nachvak Fjord. Neither of the men knew it then but this was a turning point in their lives.

I wasn't aware, in July 2009, when I heard Johan Adrian Jacobsen's name for the very first time, that this moment was also a turning point in my life. I was sitting in the library of the *Lyubov Orlova*, a Russian cruise ship sailing along the Labrador coast. A few days earlier, before landing in Hebron, I had met another passenger, Hans-Ludwig Blohm, who told me about a book, *The Diary of Abraham Ulrikab*, written by his friend Professor Hartmut Lutz. With the help of his students from the University of Greifswald, Hartmut had translated into English the diary of a Labrador Inuk who, along with his family, had been exhibited in zoos throughout Europe in 1880. Hans' summary of their travels, and of their death in Germany and Paris, intrigued me. As soon as the occasion presented itself, I picked up the copy Hans had donated to the ship's library.

My first reading of the book both shocked and fascinated me. But it struck me that there was a chapter missing. The one describing the events that unfolded in Paris where five of the eight Inuit had died. The book was silent about what had happened in the French capital.

On board the ship, Hans and I met Zipporah Nochasak, a Labrador Inuk whose family originates from Hebron, and has the same name as Nuggasak, the first of the eight Inuit to have died in Europe. Zipporah had read *The Diary of Abraham Ulrikab* shortly before boarding the ship, and she was very upset. My mother tongue being French, I promised Hans and Zipporah that, when time allowed, I would search for information about what happened to the Inuit in Paris. I figured there must have been been newspaper articles about them. If I could at least uncover where they had been buried, it might bring some sense of closure to their descendants.

Fig. 3 Hans Blohm and France Rivet.
(Photo: Micheline Leblanc, 2009)

Hans put me in touch with his friend Hartmut Lutz as well as with a German couple he had met on board the ship who were familiar with Abraham's story. They had started their own research in Germany. Through them I heard of the existence of a digitized copy of Jacobsen's 1880 diary, and of an unpublished English translation kept at Memorial University in St. John's, Newfoundland and Labrador (see Bruckner 1987).

The first time I read the diary, Jacobsen didn't appear as a very sympathetic person. It was mind-blowing to me that he would attend Paingu's autopsy and dare take her skullcap, wrap it in paper, put it in his luggage and carry it with him from Krefeld [spelled Crefeld in 1880], Germany, to Paris. Jacobsen also appeared to me as extremely selfish to think of going to a spa just a few hours after the death of the last survivor of the group of eight. He had brought these people from Labrador to Europe, had forgotten to have them vaccinated, witnessed their death and he was thinking of taking it easy at a spa! My first reaction was one of disbelief. But it was also what prompted me to want to translate Hartmut's book to French. The French-speaking community in Canada and in France needed to know about this story. But first, I needed to put my researcher's hat on so that we could add the Paris chapter to the story.

An Unexpected Find in Paris

It wasn't until the summer of 2011 that I actually was able to find new information about the group in Paris. One of the articles confirmed that Jacobsen had indeed brought a skullcap to Paris. It was shown to the members of the *Société d'anthropologie de Paris* on January 6, 1881. Another article was about plaster casts being made of the brains of Abraham, his wife Ulrike, and 20-year-old Tobias. The casts had also been presented to the members of the *Société d'anthropologie de Paris*. These two articles prompted me to send emails to museums in Paris asking if, by any chance, they would have these items in their collection.

An answer came the next morning from the *Muséum national d'histoire naturelle*. To my astonishment, not only did the museum have the skullcap in its biological anthropological collection, it also had the fully mounted skeletons of the five Inuit who died in Paris in January 1881, including Abraham's. Needless to say, my jaw dropped to the floor. Never in my wildest dreams did the thought of finding the human remains of the Labrador Inuit cross my mind.

As you can imagine, on that day, September 28, 2011, my research took a totally different path. Its purpose was no longer merely to uncover new information about the past, but it could potentially change history.

On January 8, 1881, the eve of being admitted to the Saint-Louis Hospital in Paris, Abraham wrote:

> *I do not long for earthly possessions but this is what I long for: to see my relatives again.*

A door had just opened to make this return a reality. For the last 130 years, everybody had taken for granted that the Inuit's remains had been buried and had vanished. Yet, all this time, their bones had been waiting in a museum's collections. Abraham and the other Inuit would not be coming home on their own two feet, but more than a century later, bringing back their remains was the way to grant their wishes.

In February 2012, when I met with Johannes Lampe, then Nunatsiavut's Minister of Culture, Recreation and Tourism, and Dave Lough, Deputy Minister, they made it clear that Abraham's story was an important one to tell. But, before they could inform their community that the human remains had been located, they needed to know all details pertaining to their story. After 131 years, it seemed life had picked me as the person to learn of the presence of their bones in Paris so, I made it my mission to fully research the story.

There were a few hurdles along the way, but by far, it has been a most rewarding experience. It allowed me, not only to follow the traces of the Labrador Inuit but also those of Johan Adrian Jacobsen, all the way up to the island of Risøya, where he was born, raised, and died. I must admit that he now holds a much dearer place in my heart than when I first read the English translation of his diary.

English and French translations of Johan Adrian Jacobsen's diary

When Hartmut Lutz heard that I was considering a French translation of Abraham's diary, he recommended his sister-in-law, Jacqueline Thun, for the job. Jacqueline accepted the challenge with enthusiasm. As Jacqueline and I were progressing, it became more and more obvious that it was also mandatory to translate Jacobsen's diary. Hartmut volunteered to do the English translation. The 1987 translation held at Memorial University was clearly marked as "not for publication" and, after making some comparison with the original manuscript, Hartmut deemed it incomplete.

For several months, Hartmut and Jacqueline worked on their translations independently but, spent long hours discussing their interpretations of Jacobsen's chaotic German.

In July 2013, the three of us met for the very first time at the *Museum für Völkerkunde* (now the *Museum am Rothenbaum –Kulturen und Künste der Welt*) in Hamburg where the original diary is preserved. Since the digitized images we had received from Memorial University had some unreadable parts, we were hoping to look at the original diary to finalize the translations. Unfortunately, in 2013, Jacobsen's archives were closed to researchers except for the five percent or so that had been digitized. Luckily, his 1880 and 1881 diaries were part of this selection and the museum's digitized images were of much better quality. So, Hartmut, Jacqueline, and I spent a few hours in the library trying to figure out the missing pieces.

Fig. 4 France Rivet, Hartmut Lutz, and Jacqueline Thun.
Museum am Rothenbaum – Kulturen und Künste der Welt. (Photo: Jantje Bruns, 2013)

As I was continuing the research and gathering as many 19th-century documents as possible, it became obvious that I would not be able to include the integrity of the translations in the book I was preparing on the Inuit's story. Yet, Jacobsen's diary deserved to be accessible to any scholar or person interested in his life. Hartmut and Jacqueline had dedicated so much time and effort to the translation, they deserved to hold a tangible proof of their hard work. That's when I decided to publish the first edition of *Voyage with the Labrador Eskimos, 1880–1881* (and *Voyage avec les Eskimos du Labrador, 1880–1881* for the French version). I wanted it to be ready for March 2014, when Hartmut was in Ottawa for a very short visit. We met at the Ottawa airport so that I could hand him copies of the final product.

Fig. 5 Hartmut Lutz and France Rivet.
(Photo: Hans Blohm, 2014)

Accessing Johan Adrian Jacobsen's archives

In September 2014, Hartmut and I were back at the *Museum für Völkerkunde* in Hamburg for the filming of the documentary *Trapped in a Human Zoo: based on Abraham's Diary*. It is here that for the first time, Hartmut met a representative of the Labrador Inuit community, Johannes Lampe. Johannes had been mandated by the Nunatsiavut government and by the elders' committee to travel to Europe in the footsteps of the group of 1880. Both men had a very touching conversation on the importance of Abraham and Jacobsen's diaries. They were granted the privilege of holding Jacobsen's original diary, as well as a small calendar booklet. The pages were empty for the most part, except for a few dates, such as January 13, 1881, where Jacobsen wrote, "This morning at

2 o'clock Tobias died 21 years old. Tonight at 9, Abraham died 35 years old."

Fig. 6 Johannes Lampe and Hartmut Lutz.
Museum am Rothenbaum – Kulturen und Künste der Welt.
(Photo: France Rivet, 2014)

Later that afternoon, Hartmut and I were also authorized to look through the original documents that were part of Jacobsen's correspondence. In the year between our two visits, and because of an increased number of requests from various researchers, the museum library staff had gone through a major effort to catalogue the Jacobsen Fonds and were about to reopen it to researchers. In the couple of hours at our disposal, Hartmut and I were able to identify a dozen or so letters received in 1880–1881 containing a reference to the group of Labrador Inuit. Yet, there were still quite a few boxes of material to go through (newspaper clippings, cards, invoices, …). Even the box marked as 'various documents' might hold something of interest. We knew that Jacobsen had the last wills that Abraham and Tobias wrote at the St. Louis Hospital in

Paris. He brought them with him when he visited a Moravian missionary in Bremen in May 1881. Could the wills be in this box?

Fig. 7 Hartmut Lutz reading a letter from Carl Hagenbeck.
Museum am Rothenbaum – Kulturen und Künste der Welt. (Photo: France Rivet, 2014)

I had to wait until my third round of research in Hamburg to find out. In April 2015, I was back at the museum's library. The Inuktitut wills were nowhere to be found; nothing relevant either in the newspaper clippings. But, after two whole days of digging, I had a dozen more letters relating to Jacobsen's travels with the Labrador Inuit. The most unexpected document was a tiny piece of paper with a prescription written in French, dated January 3, 1881, and signed by Dr. Panneval, the physician in charge of the Jardin d'acclimatation where the Inuit were exhibited in Paris.

A friend, pharmacist Gilles Pelletier, helped me read the prescription. It consisted mainly of antimony, gum arabic, Sydenham's laudanum, ipecacuanha syrup and powder. His opinion was that it was most likely for either food poisoning, or for an illness having symptoms similar to those of leishmaniasis (a disease caused by parasites which presents itself with skin ulcers). We still don't know whether it was meant for the Inuit who had just been vaccinated against smallpox two days earlier, or for Jacobsen who had been suffering from intermittent fever and various other symptoms for several months. But I was amazed that such a document had been preserved.

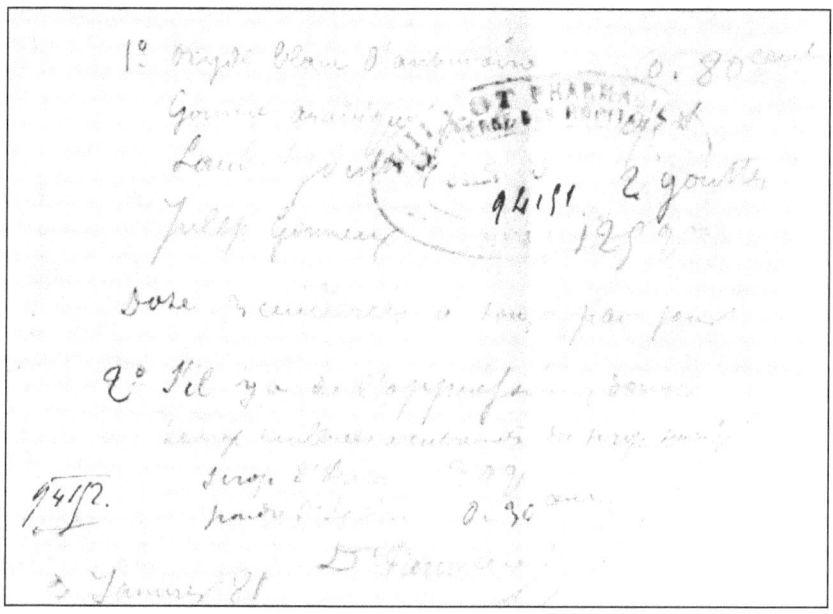

Fig. 8 January 3, 1881, prescription by Dr. Panneval.
(*Museum am Rothenbaum – Kulturen und Künste der Welt*, JAC_2_1_1)

Dieter Riedel's contributions

After my return home, I happened to talk to a friend, Doreen Larsen Riedel, whose German-born husband Dieter regularly translates German, Russian, Norwegian, or Danish texts into English. She was quick to tell me that Jacobsen's correspondence is the type of documents Dieter would love to translate. Doreen knew her husband well! Even though, Dieter later admitted that he was not happy with his wife when she brought him the news of this new task, he quickly got caught up in Jacobsen's adventures and dug in with passion and enthusiasm.

Fig. 9 Dieter Riedel translating Jacobsen's correspondence.
(Photo: France Rivet, 2015)

Dieter's curiosity led him to initiate all sorts of side searches to better understand the 19th-century context and events. Thanks to him, we have the English translations of new sections of Jacobsen's diary. In the first edition, Hartmut and Jacqueline had concentrated on the core of the diary, from June 1880 to January 1881. Dieter's work now allows us to follow Jacobsen from the fall of 1879, when he first discussed the idea of buying a ship to travel and recruit a second group of 'Eskimos,' to June 1881 as he was about to leave for North America's Northwest Coast to collect for the Berlin Royal Ethnology Museum.

It is also thanks to Dieter's spirit of inquiry and initiative that the registration documents for the *Eisbär* were located in Hamburg.

The history and fate of the *Eisbär*

When the CD with the 11-page file on the ship arrived from Hamburg, I immediately took it to Dieter so that we could discover what new information it held.

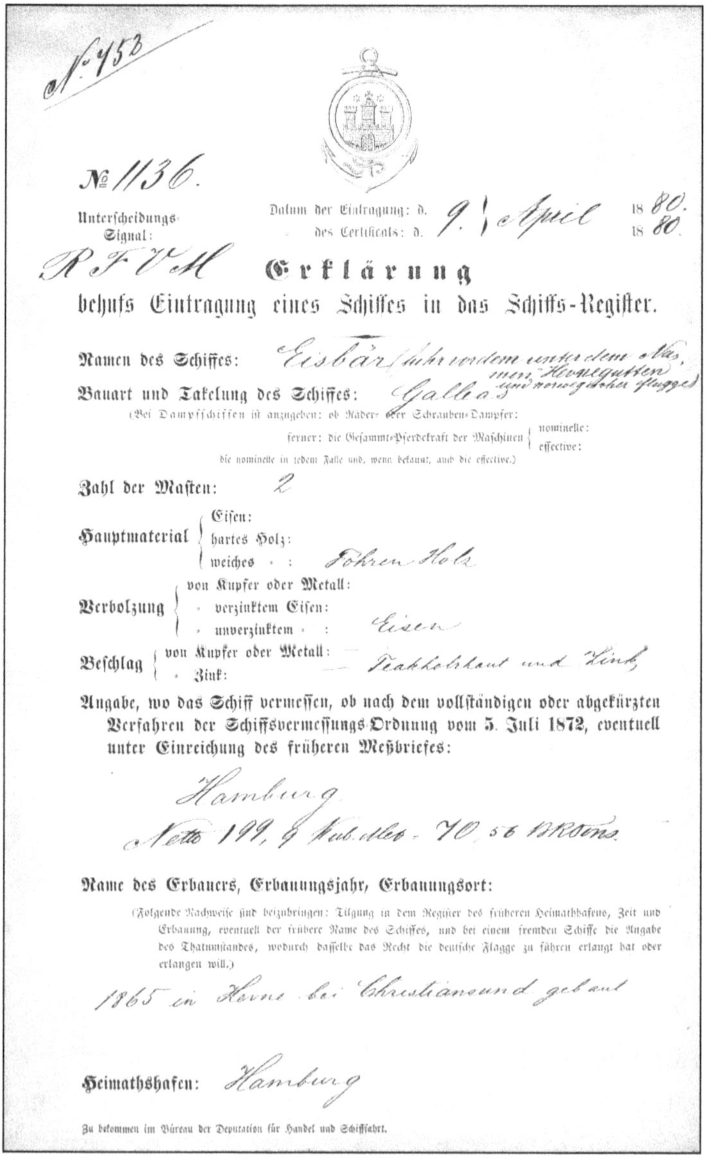

Fig. 10 Page 1 of the registration documents for the Eisbär.
(Staatsarchiv Hamburg, Seeschiffsregisternummer 1136, Source: 231-4_1203)

The two-masted 23.15 meter-long schooner made of fir wood had been built in 1865 in Hevne (now spelled Hemne), near Kristiansund, and was named *Hevnegutten* (the boy from Hevne). In his diary, Jacobsen implied that the ship was owned by himself, his brother Jacob Martin and Carl Hagenbeck. The documents show that, when registering it in Hamburg, Jacobsen agreed to Carl Hagenbeck and Jacob Martin being the sole owners with 1/3 and 2/3 of the shares respectively.

The file did not contain any drawing or photograph of the ship but the various measurements made us wonder how eight crewmen plus eight Inuit and their dogs could live comfortably during the trans-Atlantic crossing.

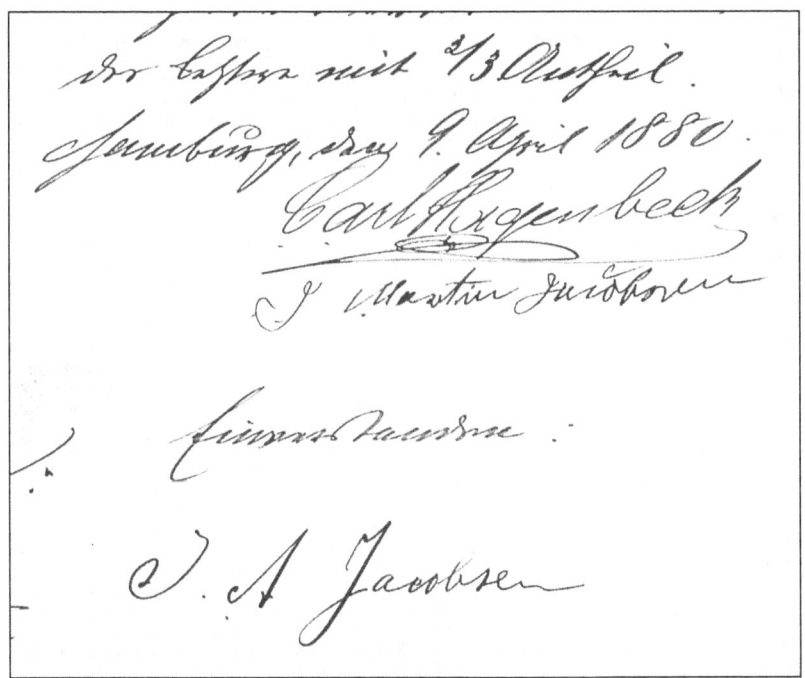

Fig. 11 Signatures on ship registration documents.
Carl Hagenbeck, Jacob Martin Jacobsen and Johan Adrian Jacobsen.
(Staatsarchiv Hamburg, Seeschiffsregisternummer 1136, Source: 231-4_1203)

The other piece of the puzzle we were able to gather from the document was that Jacob Martin Jacobsen sold the *Eisbär* in Hammerfest, Northern Norway, in 1883.

Now that the German records had revealed their secrets, Dieter and I wondered if it could be feasible to find the Norwegian records. Who did Jacobsen buy the ship from? Who was the ship builder? Who was it sold to in 1883? Where did it end its life? Where was the ship's log book? We had so many unanswered questions.

The first step was to write to the Norwegian National Archives. Their offices in Trondheim and Oslo confirmed that ship registries in Norway started in 1903, so they couldn't really help with finding the 1879 and 1883 transactions. As for who the previous owner was, archivist Jostein Molde in Trondheim offered an avenue to explore: Saras Michael Ideus Lossius (1833–1901), a Kristiansund merchant and town board member, owned a ship called *Hevnegutten* although the time frame of his ownership was unknown. So far, no progress has been made on that front and further research will have to wait for eventual visits to the Norwegian Maritime Museum in Oslo, and to the Nordmøre Museum in Kristiansund.

In June 2016, I was invited to Tromsø to participate in a two-day workshop titled *Johan Adrian Jacobsen: Collector of People and Things* organized by the Tromsø University Museum. I couldn't have asked for a better opportunity to go dig into the archives. Following the workshop, the organizer Cathrine Baglo dedicated a whole day to help me conduct research on the *Eisbär*. We started at the library of the Norwegian Polar Institute. Through their database of vessels, chief librarian Ivar Stokkeland, quickly brought up the record of a ship named *Eisber*, owned by Adrian

Jacobsen. The history simply read: "1885: Shipwrecked. Location: Whilst sealing."

The record showed that the source of the information included the 1885 custom records as well as a newspaper article. Cathrine and I spent the rest of the day at the Tromsø Regional State Archives, and at the Culture and Social Science Library of the Arctic University of Norway, going through microfilmed newspapers as well as the customs records between 1883 and 1885 for Hammerfest.

Fig. 12 Cathrine Baglo searching custom records.
(Photo: France Rivet, 2016)

We were able to recreate parts of the history of the last two years of the ship. The *Eisbär* arrived in Hammerfest from Hamburg on May 24, 1883, with Captain Stuberg[1] at the wheel. From that point on until the ship departed for its final voyage in the summer of 1885, Johan Adrian's brother Hans became the ship's captain.

The *Eisbär* sank in the summer of 1885 while sealing near Svalbard. The loss of the ship was reported in the August 25, 1885, issue of the newspaper *Finmarksposten*. Fortunately, all crew members were saved and brought back to Hammerfest on other fishing vessels.

Greenland Archives

Another aspect of the story which had never been the subject of any research was Jacobsen's recruitment attempt in Greenland in July 1880. In his diary, Jacobsen anxiously awaits the governor's reply to his request to recruit people and to collect artefacts in Jakobshavn. Couldn't the exchange between the two men be stored in archival boxes?

An email to the Qeqertarsuaq Museum where the governor was located in 1880 redirected me to Mrs. Inge Seiding, archivist at the Greenland National Archives and Museum in Nuuk. In her enthusiastic reply, Inge had already gone to the ship registry records and confirmed that the *Eisbär* was indeed in Jakobshavn harbour from July 7 to 21, 1880. Since Inge was so familiar with the archival material I needed to go through, she volunteered to spend a bit of time digging out the relevant documents. Within a week, I had received the digitized copies of 1) the letter from Governor T. S. Krarup Smith in Godhavn to Jacobsen; 2) his letter to the trade manager in Jakobshavn instructing him how to handle Jacobsen's requests, and 3) his letter to the head office of the Royal Greenland Trading Company (KGH - *Kongelige Grønlandske Handel*) in Copenhagen about Jacobsen's arrival and visits.

But what was missing was Jacobsen's initial request to the governor. Inge knew where to find it! Governor Krarup Smith had written in his letter to Copenhagen that he was including Jacobsen's letter. Therefoere, Jacobsen's letter had to be in the

KGH archives at the Danish National Archives, *Rigsarkivet*, in Copenhagen. Of course, Inge was right. Adam Jon Kronegh, an archivist at the Danish National Archives, found the file sent by the governor, photographed the documents, and emailed them to me.

Of course, there are still some pieces of the puzzle missing. Chances that they will all be uncovered are very slim, and since I do not speak the languages that would allow me to uncover them easily, I'm leaving it up to other curious researchers to continue the task.

Five years after the publication of the first edition of *Voyage with the Labrador Eskimos, 1880–1881*, I'm the first one surprised to see that this second version has gone from 88 pages to over 290! This the result of incredible cooperation and team work from people and organizations on both sides of the Atlantic Ocean.

What makes me very proud is that all this work will not only allow the Labrador Inuit to better understand the events that resulted in the death of eight of their countrymen, but it will also bring to the Jacobsen family a chapter of their history that they were not aware of.

Meeting Descendants of the Jacobsen Family

When I look back on these years of research, some of the most precious moments that come to mind are those I shared with members of the Jacobsen family. The first one was in November 2013 in Tromsø.

My visit above the Arctic Circle had two purposes: to see the temporary exhibit *Johan Adrian Jacobsen: Captain, Ethnographer and Author* presented at the Polar Museum, and to meet with Kirsten

Katharina Barton Holiman, the author of the first thesis and biography dedicated Jacobsen, and her husband Kenth Thomas Mikalsen, a descendant of one of Johan Adrian's brothers.

Fig. 13 Portraits of J. A. Jacobsen and his wife.
Temporary exhibit, Polar Museum, Tromsø. (Photo: France Rivet, 2013)

Kirsten Katharina explained that her desire to write her thesis on Jacobsen came from her fascination to hear members of her husband's family talk about this great uncle who had travelled the world. During WWII, after his house in Hamburg had been bombed, 90-year-old Jacobsen returned to the island of Risøya, where he was born. Sitting in his rocking chair, he loved telling stories of his adventures.

Kirsten Katharina and Kenth spend many weekends on Risøya, the island and the house Jacobsen lived in still belong to their family. As they explained, many mementos recall Jacobsen's life. It was my turn to be fascinated. How I wished I could one day visit Risøya.

Kirsten Katharina gave me the contact information for one of Jacobsen's direct descendant, Kerstin Bedranowsky, a great-grand-daughter living in Hamburg. In the fall of 2014, as the filming of the documentary *Trapped in a Human Zoo* was taking the crew to Hamburg, I wondered if Kerstin would be willing to meet with us. It seemed that having a representative of the Labrador Inuit meet a descendant of the man who had recruited and travelled with the deceased ancestors could eventually be beneficial for the healing and reconciliation process.

Kerstin agreed to the idea and wanted to bring her father Adrian, now in his 80s. The meeting happened on September 24, 2014, at the Lindner Park-Hotel Hagenbeck in Stellingen, north of Hamburg.

When I met Adrian Jacobsen, I couldn't believe that I was sitting beside someone who had known one of the main characters of the story I had been researching for four years. It suddenly brought Johan Adrian Jacobsen so much closer.

Adrian was only nine years old in the early 1940s, before Hamburg was bombed by the allies, but he still remembered listening to his grandfather tell stories of his adventures. He showed us his family photo album, the collection of newspaper clippings his mother had started and which he later continued. You could see the pride in his eyes. Through Kerstin, acting as our German-English interpreter, Adrian explained that he had no recollection of his grandfather mentioning the Labrador Inuit. He had never heard of that chapter of his grandfather's life until I knocked on their door. He couldn't shed new light on his grandfather's feelings or thoughts about what had happened. But his smile and the sparkle in his eyes made it a most memorable discussion. It was such a privilege to witness Johannes, Adrian, and Kerstin having a friendly and joyful conversation. To see that it was feasible to put the tragic events of 1880 behind and have a heartfelt conversation was very inspiring.

Fig. 14 Johannes Lampe, Adrian Jacobsen, and Kerstin Bedranowsky. (Photo: France Rivet, 2014)

Their discussion was immortalized by the film crew. Unfortunately, the film director and producer had to make the decision not to include it in the final cut of the documentary. Nevertheless, it is registered in our minds and hearts, and, for both Johannes and I, was a highlight of our trip to Europe in the footsteps of the eight Inuit who had shared five months of their life with Jacobsen.

Visit to Risøya

A year later, when I was approached by Cathrine Baglo to take part in the *Johan Adrian Jacobsen: Collector of People and Things* workshop in Tromsø, I felt so privileged to be part of this gathering with Hartmut Lutz, Cathrine, Kirsten Katharina and four other historians, anthropologists, museum curators from Germany and the United States who had all studied different chapters of Jacobsen's life. I must admit that I had trouble containing my excitement when I read that day two would be spent visiting Risøya.

Fig. 15 Jacobsen Family house on Risøya, Norway.
(Photo: France Rivet, 2016)

Stepping onto the beach where Jacobsen first got into a boat to learn sailing; looking through the window and seeing the same mountains and sea he stared at as a young boy, dreaming about travelling the world, and as an old man reliving his many expeditions; touching the rocking chair he sat in, captivating those listening to his life's stories; looking at his picture on the wall surrounded by those of his idols, Norwegian explorers Fridtjof Nansen, Roald Amundsen, and Otto Sverdrup; eating seagull eggs which he and his family gathered by the thousands each summer; all of it made him so real. He was no longer a distant character who had lived in a past era. He was still very present in the lives of his family's descendants.

Fig. 16 Kenth Thomas Mikalsen welcoming us on Risøya.
(Photo: France Rivet, 2016)

Fig. 17 Portraits - Nansen, Amundsen, Jacobsen, and Sverdrup. Risøya.
(Photo: France Rivet, 2016)

Fig. 18 Kirsten K. Barton Holiman and Hartmut Lutz. Risøya.
(Photo: France Rivet, 2016)

Fig. 19 View from the kitchen window. Risøya.
(Photo: France Rivet, 2016)

When I started this introduction, I didn't envision writing so much. I hope that my words bring useful and meaningful insight into the various aspects of conducting historical research, especially the many unexpected rewards I was blessed with and the numerous people who shared my path to help bring this chapter of history to light.

As for the first edition, the purpose of *Voyage with the Labrador Eskimo, 1880–1881* is to make available the raw material uncovered so that it can be used by anyone who has an interest in further studying Johan Adrian Jacobsen's life. It is being published as a complement to the book *In the Footsteps of Abraham Ulrikab: The Events of 1880–1881*.

Thank you! Nakummek! Takk!

---

[1] As per her research in Norway's National Archives, Cathrine Baglo believes that Captain Stuberg is probably 'Skipper' Joachim Stuberg from the Kvalsund parish in Hammerfest. His middle name is hard to decipher.

Translators' Preliminary Remarks

By Hartmut Lutz and Dieter Riedel

This translation is based on the digitized pages of Johan Adrian Jacobsen's diary preserved and provided to us by the *Museum am Rothenbaum – Kulturen und Künste der Welt* in Hamburg.

(1) In the original manuscript, there are corrections and additions inserted between the lines or on the margins as well as on separate pages, obviously written by Jacobsen at a later time and in a more legible hand. These corrections are reflected in the translation only if they add value and help understand the text. Insertions between the lines are here reproduced $^{\text{as a superscript}}$ while the additions on the margins follow immediately the entry for the day they are meant for; they are marked 'On margin:' and appear in italics. Insertions in the diary that are added on separate pages are, in this translation, added immediately following the pages they are clipped to or inserted in. Sometimes Jacobsen underlined words or printed them or spelled them in bold—such markings are also given in the translation by underlining or using bold types, respectively.

(2) The round brackets in the translations (…) as well as the words cancelled by a ~~line~~ follow Jacobsen's original brackets and cancellations, whereas our own explanations or comments are

given in square brackets: [...] or as end of chapter notes. Translations of uncertain passages, i.e. where words are invisible, obscure, or incomplete, are given in slashes like this: /.../. Sometimes we were not sure about the reading and have added caveats and explanations in square brackets.

(3) The original text is mostly written in German with some Norwegian, English, and French words. But the spelling of words may be incorrect, and words may be written as they are pronounced in German [example: 'Stimer' = steamer]. The grammar of some sentences is unusual. But the handwriting is usually easily legible, though understanding the meaning of some words correctly, is sometimes difficult and requires some imagination.

(4) In order to ease the understanding of the text, we took some liberty to correct the spelling and syntax errors, but the phrasing still reflects Jacobsen's somewhat chaotic language.

(5) To respect the authenticity of the historical documents, we have tried to reproduce people and places names as they are spelled in the handwritten documents. This will explain why you are bound to encounter various spellings especially for the non-Christian Inuit names. You may find Nuggasak under Noggasak, Nokassak, Nogasak, etc. Paingu may appear as Paingo, Pangu, Bairngo, Bangu, Baignu, Beango, etc. while Tigianniak could be spelled Terrianiak, Teggianiack, Tiggianiak, etc.

Acknowledgments

This book would not have been possible without the collaboration of many individuals. We would like to express our gratitude to all who helped in one way or other, but specifically to:

- Cathrine Baglo (Tromsø Museum – Universitetsmuseet),
- Kirsten Katharina Barton Holiman (Arctic University of Norway – Department of Language and Culture),
- Ulf Bollmann (Staatsarchiv – Ressortbezogene Archivische Aufgaben, Hamburg),
- Jantje Bruns (Museum am Rothenbaum – Kulturen und Künste der Welt, Hamburg),
- Christina Chávez (Museum am Rothenbaum – Kulturen und Künste der Welt, Hamburg),
- Eva Dittertová (Náperstek Museum of Asian, African and American Cultures, Prague),
- Anne Kirsti Jacobsen,
- Wulf Köpke (Museum für Völkerkunde Hamburg),
- Adam Jon Kronegh (Danish National Archives, Copenhagen),
- Hartmut Lutz (emeritus, University of Greifswald),
- Kenth Thomas Mikalsen,
- Jostein Molde (Norwegian National Archives – Trondheim),
- Diane Mongeau,
- Svein-Olaf Nilssen (Norwegian National Archives – Tromsø),
- Season Osborne,
- Linda G. Ostermann (Qeqertarsuaq Museum),

- Gilles Pelletier,
- Barbara Plankensteiner (Museum am Rothenbaum – Kulturen und Künste der Welt, Hamburg),
- Anja Reimer (Ilulissat Museum),
- Dieter Riedel,
- Inge Sieding (Greenland National Archives, Nuuk),
- Ivar Stokkeland (Norsk Polarinstitutt), and
- Tone Wang (Museum of Cultural History, University of Oslo)

Johan Adrian Jacobsen's Diary

Voyage to Norway to Buy a Ship

October-December 1879

My brother [Jacob Martin] now had the idea that he wanted to get himself a vessel so that he could fish for Greenland sharks below [= south of] Iceland. I was so happy about it that I mentioned it to Hagenbeck. He thought that if we could get a vessel for that price (my brother had thought that he could get one fully equipped for 15 000 [gold] marks), then Hagenbeck would take a one-third share of it, in order that we might bring him Eskimos who would be a valuable ship's load for him. So, we began at once to look for a vessel, and went to Glückstadt,[1] [where we found one], but that vessel sailed poorly, we could not agree on the price, and so that deal fell through.

They told me that I should go to Norway and buy a galleas[2] cheaply, which we thought that one could be found. But that had no result until the middle of November. Now I was supposed to go over to Norway to buy a vessel. I left Hamburg on the 14th,[3] and landed in Stavanger. But [there], all [of the boats] were too expensive, except for one new vessel, of a man from Fjordane[4] in that city. His father had taken it to a place where ice formed so quickly that it was already frozen in by the time when he had come to see me in Stavanger. So that purchase could not be made. I then travelled to Bergen, where I found a telegram [telling me] to go to Christianssund[5] to look at a galleas which was for sale there. I had already begun to think that this enterprise was going to lead to our ruin, but my brother [Jacob Martin] who was always somewhat headstrong, asked me to forget that idea, and he would not listen to anything else. So, I had to go to Christianssund, where I arrived on the 1st of December.

> *On margin:*
> *Because during the [past] two years Hagenbeck had made /deals?/ with both Eskimos and Lapps[6] which ended with poor returns on his investments, I travelled with the ship's pilot Falke. He suggested that we should continue with that business [of ethnographic shows]. But it was always difficult for us to find the kind of folks who understood how interested the public was in them. Because, of course, in the northern half of our globe, those kinds of folks are scarce.*

> *On margin:*
> *December 1–8.*

Eight days later I had bought the galleas whose name was *Hevnegutten* [the boy from Hevne]. I immediately made a contract with the shipbuilder Darve for him to add an ice skin.[7] Because the Elbe River was frozen solid, there was no way to get the vessel over there, and anyway, there were storms from the southwest every day. I knew the Greenland shark business from [when I had lived in] Tromsø. I ordered rifles and cartridges in Christianssund, together with heavy fishing gear.

> *On margin: [The text along the left side of this page refers to the Patagonians, the group which arrived in Europe after the Labrador Inuit's death. It therefore seems that the notes on the left margins of the pages deal with events which happened at other times.]*

Throughout December, the weather was stormy with rain, which was sometimes mixed with snow, and therefore the work of installing the ice skin on the vessel went ahead only slowly.

I had Captain Bang come [to Christianssund] from Tønsberg, so that he could be appointed as skipper [of the vessel].

On margin:
Captain Bang had many years of experience in the Arctic Ocean commanding ships flying the German flag.

January 1880

In January, the work being done on the vessel in the shipyard was finished. I had arranged to transport a load of guano[8] to Hamburg, and we took the freight and supplies on board, but during one fine night, the schooner filled with water, and we had to unload more than 100 bags full of [soaking wet] guano, which had been ruined. So I had to take the vessel back to the shipyard in order to find the leak through which the water had entered. That took almost a month, and then I could no longer let the vessel sit in the harbour. In the meantime, I had to find another load of guano, because the first load had been spoiled, and that cost me over 500 [silver] kroner and a whole month of lost time.

On margin:
It was really Captain Bang who had caused this damage, because that evening he had not tested the pumps after the load had been brought on board [which caused the hull of the vessel to settle deeper into the water, and allowed water to enter through a hidden opening]. For an explanation of the cause of what happened with this vessel, see page 61 of my book Die weisse Grenze *[published by Brockhaus at Leipzig, 1931], where I described this event in more detail.*

[1] Glückstadt is a town located on the right bank of the Elbe River about 50 km northwest of Hamburg.

[2] A galleas is a two-masted coastal sailing ship.

[3] At the top of the left margin of the page is a note: The 14th of November.

[4] Jacobsen must be referring to Sogn og Fjordane, a county in southwest Norway.

[5] Christianssund is a city on the west coast of Norway. Now spelled Kristiansund.

[6] Lapplanders, an indigenous people living in the extreme North of Scandinavia. They are known today as the Sami people. (Oxford Dictionnary)

[7] By 'ice skin,' Jacobsen must mean an additional layer of planks over the hull.

[8] Guano, the excrement of seabirds or bats, is a highly effective fertilizer. In the 19th century, guano trade played a pivotal role in the development of modern farming practices. (Wikipedia)

Sailing the New Ship to Hamburg

February 18 – March 18, 1880

We finally got under way on the 18th of February. The first few days we had good wind until we came to the /Hoïder?/ Islands from the island of Utsira,[1] when the wind turned towards the west, when we saw a derelict English cutter,[2] owned by a rich Englishman who had spent the summer at Svinör[3] and who during the summer had taken lobsters over to England. It came from a voyage to Norway and had been surprised by a terrible storm which had wrecked the whole rigging and dumped it overboard, and when the owner came up onto the deck, a huge wave had swept him into the sea. The next day, a Danish schooner had rescued the other people on board [of the cutter]. We tried to tow that [abandoned] vessel, but late in the evening, before we were able to fasten a tow rope onto it, a storm began and we could not leave one of our crew on board [of the wreck], who would have been able to steer it and otherwise to control it.

Unfortunately, all of our efforts were in vain, because the westerly storm winds became so powerful that we had to cut it [the tow rope], and were forced to drift with the winds for 8 days and were at times near the Dogger[4] [Bank] and finally our petroleum ran out, and because at the same time a strong storm wind blew from the southwest, we decided to try to reach a harbour in Norway, and on the second day at noon, we anchored in Mandals Kleven.[5]

There I met an old Tromsø /man?/, a son of /Oscaar?/ from Lyngen.⁶ He was there with a brig which he skippered and which had to go to Scotland. We became good friends; [it was] too bad that we could not remember [ever] having met each other at home. And I have to confess that most Norwegians whom I have met so far in my wandering about, have been of a very different kind. I don't want to speak ill of the people of my country, but I do not trust them much. We stayed three days at Kleven and then on the 6th we left in very good but unsafe weather, because it soon turned into a southeasterly storm which soon changed into a storm coming from the west but then we were disappointed because it soon turned towards the southeast so that we had to cruise up and down [the North Sea] a whole 3 degrees East, and got near Heligoland.⁷

Finally, on the 18th we got to Hamburg, but at Cuxhaven⁸ I lost some time, because the tide had just gone out.

---

[1] Utsira is a small island northwest of Stavanger.

[2] A cutter is a small fore-and-aft rigged sailing boat with one mast, more than one headsail, and a running bowsprit, used as a fast auxiliary. (Oxford Dictionnary)

[3] Jacobsen is either referring to a Norwegian island and a former port in southern Norway, which has now been replaced by Vigeland, or to a community on the Swedish coast in the northern Baltic Sea.

[4] A large sandbank in a shallow area of the North Sea about 100 kilometres off the east coast of England.

[5] Mandal is the southernmost community of Norway. It was famous for its shipbuilding activities. Nearby, on the island of Gismerøya, the natural harbour of Kleven was one of northern Europe's best harbours.

[6] A municipality in the Troms county, in Northern Norway, where Jacobsen grew up.

[7] Heligoland is a small German archipelago in the North Sea near the mouth of the Elbe River.

[8] Cuxhaven is a town situated on the shore of the North Sea at the northwestern end of the mouth of the Elbe River.

In Hamburg for Outfitting

March 18 – 23, 1880

At that time my ship would have been ready to leave for the open sea, if everything had gone as planned, but many changes still had to be made to that vessel. We had deregistered it from the *Norsk Veritas*,[1] but now we had to re-register it with them again, but first we had to replace the broken mizzen [centre] mast as well as the mizzen boom, very many ropes, and the sails had to be checked, in short, there was a lot of work to do.

We equipped the ship for three different purposes: fishing for Greenland sharks, hunting hooded seals and whales. All that took some doing, and then there were other things which had to be added. In short, when everything was done, the fully equipped ship cost 28 000 [gold] marks instead of the 15 000 [gold] marks which had been calculated. And in addition, when the ship finally was ready, we still had not secured any freight for it, nor could we keep [Captain] Bang as skipper, because the ship now was flying the German flag and had German owners.

March 24, 1880

I had to make a trip to Berlin in order to finally get permission to leave. Before we hired Captain Bang, we had considered another skipper from Tønsberg, named Gulliksen.[2] He too had once been in charge of ships sailing for the Polar Company, and he was a steady, suitable man [so we appointed him] as First Mate. And then there was Christensen, who had also skippered vessels in the Arctic Ocean for many years. In addition we also had a navigator on board. So the skip was well prepared, but by now it was so late that we could not think of any plan to be able to fish for anything. So, we thought of getting some wild and some tame Eskimos instead.

On margin:
Because we had that leak in the vessel at Kristiansund, and we had to return to the shipyard there, and because of the strong storms in the North Sea which came from the wrong direction, our voyage was frustrated.

The year 1880 was certainly the year in which I had the least luck in my whole long life. Everything which I had wanted to do went wrong. I just had no luck with everything that I had wanted to /accomplish?/ in my native land.

---

[1] The *Norsk Veritas* was founded in Norway in 1864 to head technical inspection and evaluation of Norwegian merchant vessels. It is still in operation today under the name DNV GN. (Wikipedia)

[2] Cathrine Baglo remarks that the Norwegian archives show no skipper named Gulliksen in Tønsberg, but several from the neighbouring community of Nøtterøy.

Fig. 20 Hamburg Harbour, 1883.
(Photo by Georg Koppmann. Wikimedia Commons)

Fig. 21 Map of Jacobsen's 1880 travels in Greenland and Labrador.
(Illustration: Diane Mongeau)

SAILING TO GREENLAND ON THE *EISBÄR*

Here I have started [to write] my journal in the German language. That is to say, such as I write it.

Tuesday • April 27, 1880

On the 27th of April we were finally at the stage that the voyage could begin. The pilot arrived at 2 o'clock in the afternoon, at the same time as a steamer tug. My brother [Jacob Martin] and my sister-in-law [Henny][1] accompanied us to Brunshausen,[2] where we had to anchor, because there was already a strong tidal current. Here we said our last goodbyes. My brother and [his] wife went back to Hamburg, and we began to move with the ebb tide. [The water and air were?] quiet, and we drifted with the current.

Wednesday • April 28, 1880

At 1 o'clock, we anchored again. But already at 3 o'clock, a good breeze began to blow from the east, the anchor was lifted again, and at 7 o'clock, we anchored above Cuxhaven. The current of the tide was so extremely strong that we did not dare to leave the ship until 11 o'clock in order to get the ship's pilot back onto land. In fact the ebb tide was still so forceful that we went ahead only very cautiously to reach Cuxhaven.

Thursday • April 29, 1880

At 1 o'clock, we came back on board. Towards 9 o'clock, we lifted the anchor and steered for the sea, with a good breeze from the northeast. At 3 o'clock, we passed Heligoland.

Friday • April 30, 1880

After supper there was a weak NW[3] wind and then it turned to the opposite direction. That is not a good omen for such a long voyage as we have to make. On board we are working busily to make the ship sea-worthy. We are heading towards the NE.

> *On margin:*
> *As mentioned earlier, we had first thought that our plan would be that on the east coast of Greenland we would catch as many seals as we could, and that then in West Greenland we would try to persuade a couple of Eskimo families to travel with us to Germany. If we did not succeed in West Greenland, then we would try in southern Baffinland.*[4]

Saturday • May 1, 1880

Wind from the NW, light breeze under cloud-covered sky. We now are heading WSW, but make no progress. We do not get ahead. Otherwise everything is well on board.

Sunday • May 2, 1880

During the morning there was no wind. Towards noon, a slight breeze from the SE. Towards evening, the wind turned eastward, and there was a bit more breeze.

Monday • May 3, 1880

NE wind. Fresh breeze. Now it is a useless breeze—the ship lies sideways to the wind.

Tuesday • May 4, 1880

NE wind with a fresh breeze, towards evening, it decreased, while the wind turned towards the north. It is continuously foggy.

Wednesday • May 5, 1880

NNE wind; fresh breeze, and towards evening, a feeble breeze. At noon we had reached a position of 57° 47' N, 1° 17' W.[5]

Thursday • May 6, 1880

NW wind. During the morning we made the topsail fast and reefed the mainsail. During the afternoon, we also reefed the mizzen [sail]. Frequent rain showers.

Friday • May 7, 1880

Storm from the NW, with rain showers or hail showers; the waves begin to mount. 50° 1' N, 1° 53' [W].

Saturday • May 8, 1880

Breeze from the north. We head towards the west. It is rather sad to have head winds day after day. No advance [progress].

Sunday • May 9, 1880

Unsteady northerly wind, during the afternoon, NW with rain showers, at noon, rising waves are running against us. No hope of getting ahead.

Monday • May 10, 1880

Variable NNW wind, at times quite still. At noon, our position was 60° 18' N, 2° 14' [W].

Tuesday • May 11, 1880

NE wind, a beautiful breeze. Now for the first time we were able to maintain our course after so much headwind. At 4 o'clock, we passed Shetland's northeastern point, [having gone] a distance of 28 minutes in a straight line.

Wednesday • May 12, 1880

Easterly wind, beautiful weather with a light breeze. The ship had slowly moved 15 degrees by noon.

Thursday • May 13, 1880

A slight breeze from the east. We are able to see the Faroe Islands. During the afternoon, we were three miles off towards the south, and then the wind stopped completely. [The water] is too deep to think of fishing.

Friday • May 14, 1880

It was still throughout the day. We fished at a depth of about 80 to

100 fathoms.⁶ I caught a (~~wolffish~~) ᴴᵃˡⁱᵇᵘᵗ of at least 100 pounds as well as a smaller one. The others also caught some smaller fish. Towards evening, the current carried us off the fishing ground.

I went out in a small boat and shot 20 small ˡᵃᵘᵍʰⁱⁿᵍ gulls /(Tadderot)/. I also shot a sea parrot [puffin] and an Arctic gull, all of which I stuffed.

Saturday • May 15, 1880

We are always floating without movement; now it is becoming boring; there is nothing to shoot at. And we are also too far away from that fishing ground. [The lead line] cannot reach the sea bottom. To entertain themselves the crew members played with the barrel organ.

Sunday • May 16, 1880

Rain with variable breezes, at times still. We are now headed in a westerly direction away from the Faroe Islands. We are moving ahead awfully slowly and do not seem to have any luck.

Monday • May 17, 1880

Northerly wind. Towards evening, it turned into a very weak westerly breeze. 61° 13' N, 9° 2' W.

Tuesday • May 18, 1880

WSW wind. The ship runs on course at a good speed, but in spite of that, the ship is headed sharply into the wind.

Wednesday • May 19, 1880

Westerly winds. A fresh breeze. The waves are beginning to mount, and it looks as if a storm is about to begin.

Thursday • May 20, 1880

Storm from the NW with high waves. At 5 o'clock, we changed course towards the SW and used only the small sails.

Friday • May 21, 1880

Continuing storm from the NW. We are heading into the storm towards the SW. There is absolutely no way to make any progress.

Saturday • May 22, 1880

NNW breeze which is weakening, but terrible waves. The movement of the waves is such that the sails could not maintain the ship's course. Fine rain with fog.

Sunday • May 23, 1880

The wind was quite variable, and veered from westerly to northerly. Towards evening, it was completely quiet with big waves from the NW. I caught a so-called /Cape chicken?/ which I skinned and prepared.

Monday • May 24, 1880

Quiet the whole day with very big waves coming from the west. We had to furl our sails and I was affected by the lateral movements of the ship.

Tuesday • May 25, 1880

During the last few days I was not well. My head was always empty. It's getting worse from day to day so that I fear I am becoming sick. The whole day was quiet til the evening then we had a weak easterly breeze with snow showers and big waves.

Wednesday • May 26, 1880

Easterly wind with fresh breeze. Rainy. At noon, we had reached 62° 26' N, 23° 19' W. I am now so sick that I have to lie in bed. It is a cold fever. I cannot eat anything but I always have a tremendous thirst. Part of the problem is that we have so little wood and coal that I cannot light a fire. It is very damp and cold in my cabin in this wet weather.

> *On margin:*
> *Because we had filled our wooden barrel in Hamburg with water from the Elbe River which served as ballast, we lost much of that water [through leakage] that the water drips from the walls in the cabin.*

Thursday • May 27, 1880

NE wind with snow showers. Stormy. During the afternoon, NNE [winds] decreasing speed with storm. 62° 31' N, 26° 4' W.

Friday • May 28, 1880

Weak NE breezes. Toward noon it became quiet. During the afternoon, SW wind with breezes. I have to remain in bed and can only drink some water.

Saturday • May 29, 1880

A beautiful breeze from SSW. Afternoon, it [the wind] turned toward south. At 8 o'clock, we saw the snowy mountains of Iceland towards the SE. I had to go to the deck despite my misery in order to see the Snejökel[7] mountain. It is part of a mountain range which rises to a height of 5 to 6 000 feet but viewed from the sea, right up to the top everything was covered with snow. Its name really describes its nature.

> *On margin:*
> *I suffered from cold fever with severe diarrhea. Some amongst the crew suffered from rheumatism and of swollen joints.*

Sunday • May 30, 1880

Easterly breeze. We sighted a Norwegian steamer hunting seals, and at 12 o'clock midnight, we saw ice. I feel worse every day and have to stay in bed. ([At noon] I was unable to determine our position [with the sextant].)

Monday • May 31, 1880

Considerably stronger breeze, or rather a *kuling*.[8] We were in [we went on board of] the Norwegian ship, and its captain, Carsten Brun, came on board and brought along a good dose of quinine,[9] because our people let him know [that I was ill] when they first went on board [of his ship]. We saw many sealing ships which had stopped here to watch for hooded seals. Most of them carried a good catch from Jan Maien [Island].[10]

We steered again away from the edge of the ice, and in the direction of Iceland, and soon saw 3 ships catching harp seals towards the west from the last ones we had seen. Our lead line reached 190 fathoms, but a huge current ^(strong easterly) [which may have carried the line with it] and we did not reach bottom.

Tuesday • June 1, 1880

The currents always ran eastward and so fast that it was impossible [to use a lead line] to reach the [sea] bottom. Nor do we get any fish. 66° N, 25° 58' W.

Wednesday • June 2, 1880

Always the same endless current; impossible to reach the [sea] bottom. Today, we saw 6 sealing steamers because we sit close to the edge of the [pack] ice. At 9 o'clock in the morning, we began to lift the warp [heave up the anchor], but now happened what I had always feared: the warp bar was too heavy, and one could heave it up only one way: by using a line, and therefore it took 5 hours in order to heave up the warp. This warp and anchor really need a very powerful winch.

By 6 o'clock [p.m.], we were again among ice.

Thursday • June 3, 1880

Slight breeze from the south. We were surrounded by ice. Towards evening, the fog lifted, and we found ourselves in thick ice not far from the open sea. At 7 o'clock, [Captain] Bang shot a male harp seal. Unfortunately, I was too sick to go onto the deck. Otherwise I would have asked Bang to carefully skin the seal so it could be properly prepared and stuffed. Unfortunately, I was not aware of this, and therefore the animal was skinned in the usual manner, and the skeleton was left on the ice. I have to confess that I was very sorry after that.

Friday • June 4, 1880

Slight SW [breeze]. During the afternoon, [Captain] Bang went on board of the [Norwegian] brig *Narnen* from Christiania.[11] It is a sailing ship, and it had been lucky, for at the beginning of April near [the island of] Jan Maien it had taken on a load of 10 barrels of textiles and food. Several of the people on that ship were sick. The captain and his son visited us. Unfortunately, we had no letters ready, because [their ship] will soon go back home.

> *On margin:*
> *As I had learned to some extent the preparation of animals [taxidermy] from Mr. Umlauff[12] in Hamburg, I wanted to do as much taxidermy as possible. But my sickness prevented that.*
>
> *I sent one letter with the [S.S.] Harald Harfagre [to] Captain [Carsten] Brun.*

Saturday • June 5, 1880

Light breeze from WSW with very foggy air, during the evening almost no wind. We have given up trying to hunt bearded seals and are now moving along the edge of the ice. It is impossible to meet any bearded seals. I have said that we wasted ˢᵖᵉⁿᵗ 14 days trying to do that.

But now we need to change course towards the Davis Strait, because we still have a long way to go. I can see quite well that it is useless for us to try to hunt bearded seals here, for without wind one cannot get anywhere. And most days are foggy, so any day with sunshine seems like a miracle, and then along comes a storm with big waves, and one gets driven far away from the ice. For several days a storm caused a terrible movement of the ice. And in addition, the wind and waves packed the ice together so much [and so high] that one never could see for any great distance. And when the ice is in such movement, the bearded seals never go onto it. In short, with a sailing ship it is at best possible for only one day each week to go along the ice in order to keep it in sight [and look for seals]. Recently, in March, the bark *Narnen*, a sailing ship, [was here] to look for seals. That ship is well and strongly built, but it got only 300 bearded seals.

While the Norwegian steamer which had just arrived, had already several thousand [seals], the same brig *Narnen*, which had been in [this] place since the beginning of May, had not been able to get a single one here, while in contrast near Jan Maien it had made a good catch.

Sunday • June 6, 1880

Easterly breeze. Went along the ice towards the west. Big waves from the west. In the afternoon, a storm; we reefed [the sails].

Monday • June 7, 1880

We always kept close to the ice in spite of the storm. I am now beginning to get a bit better. I can eat some soup. I am terribly debilitated and so weak that I can hardly remain standing. I keep taking quinine regularly. 64° 4' N, 30° 49' W.

Tuesday • June 8, 1880

Today, beautiful weather with a nice breeze. Early in the morning we passed by ice floes with some harp seal mothers and their young, but we continued on our way. We were very busy trying to reach the edge of the fast ice,[13] but by noon we had gone as far as we could. We again saw several bearded seals, and we immediately made a boat ready and tried to get to them, but all of them had ^already returned to the water before the boat could get close enough to them to shoot them. But a young harp seal lay on an ice floe quite close to our ship.

[Today] I felt so well as I had not felt in a long time, probably because of the effect of the sunshine. I had the small boat launched and went out and killed [the seal]. I had the skin prepared [by the crew] because I hoped that we might [be able] to spot both female and male [seals], and to then make up a family group. But that proved to be a vain hope, because no males were caught. The boat came back later and brought back two adult females and 4 young seals.

I had the two adults prepared [by crew members] so that they could be stuffed later. Towards the evening, we saw 6 steamers which had penetrated far into the ice, and it seemed to us that they had made a good catch, because some of them still moved around to collect their catch. During the evening, it began to blow, and it became necessary for us to get away from the ice.

On margin:
When our big boat was among the ice, I went out in our small boat and shot the young bearded seal, because I wanted to stuff it.

Wednesday • June 9, 1880

Westerly storm. We cruised along near the ice. The waves had become bigger. 65° 21' N, 31° 58' W.

Thursday • June 10, 1880

During the night the wind became southeasterly and then developed into a strong gale. We could only use our smallest sails.

Friday • June 11, 1880

Before noon, the gale began to weaken. We kept cruising in the open sea. During the afternoon, we saw the coast of eastern Greenland about 10 miles away. It consisted of high mountains, and two fjords could also be seen. 65° 14' N, 33° W.

On margin:
We were located somewhat north of the Eskimo settlement of Angmagssalik.[14]

Saturday • June 12, 1880

Until noon it was quiet. Small ice floes drifted everywhere. Then we could see the edge of the fast ice from a distance. During the evening, there was a slight easterly breeze. With a fresh breeze from the east, we headed towards land. There was a bay in the ice which extended for several miles towards the land, and we finally thought that it would be free of ice right up to the shore. But about 5 miles off [the land], we met the edge of the really fast ice. It did not seem possible to penetrate through it, but it is difficult to judge whether a steamship [might do that]. And just then there was also a thick fog, so that we could not tell how much the ice had been piled up. We could see several deep fjords, or at least it looked like that. The mountains along the coast were very high, I estimated them to be 6 000 to 7 000 feet [above sea level; about 1 800 to 2 000 metres]. They were still covered by a layer of snow almost right down to the sea. It was difficult for us to find our way out of that bay again, but we had a good fresh breeze. At noon: 65° 32' N, 34° W.

Sunday • June 13, 1880

In the morning, we were free of the ice, and I can see that one day we will reach the Davis Strait. We now begin to sail towards it. We therefore let the ship run all day WSW. We had a light breeze coming from the NE.

Monday • June 14, 1880

The wind now turned towards the NW, and the air became hazy. We have set all of our sails, and we slowly make our way forward. At noon: 61° 39' N, 37° 16' W.

Tuesday • June 15, 1880

During the early morning, the wind was from the SW. During the afternoon, we had a possibly slightly stronger breeze, which we needed badly. But towards evening, the wind calmed again, and we had fog and rain. 61° 39' N, 37° 16' W.[15]

Wednesday • June 16, 1880

Mostly calm. Easterly breeze with rain and fog. During the afternoon, SSW with big waves and a lot of rain. 60° 12' N, 37° 35' W.

Thursday • June 17, 1880

Variable SE wind with much rain and fog. In that kind of weather, people along with everything else, tend to rot. Water drips from the skylight, the stovepipe is broken, and the stove does not work either. I wish that we had proper coal, but all of it which we had in the hold is used up, and the rest was stowed on top of the ship's keel [beam], and it will take a couple of days' work to make a passage to where it is. That can happen only later in the Davis Strait where the sea is often quiet. I am also feeling worse since this unpleasant weather started. Ever since we left the Faroe Islands, we never had three sunny days in a row. Of all of my voyages in the Arctic, none has been as depressing, and I have hated none as much as this one. Perhaps that is because I am sick, and because ahead of me I only see ruin. I have never feared the future as I do this year.

Friday • June 18, 1880

A strong wind from the east with much rain and fog, and big waves coming from the northeast.

We have had to make a big circle around Cape Farewell,[16] and although we sailed a long way, we just sailed around it. 58° 4' N, 39° 22' W.

Saturday • June 19, 1880

Easterly wind, at times stormy with very high waves from the NE. We now have the wind blowing towards the side of the ship so that we can use only small sails. The ship rolls strongly from side to side, but that is not surprising. It rains without interruption; even at the equator I have rarely seen more rain, except that here the rain is finer. Today, I have had the stovepipe repaired enough so that this evening I was able to make a little fire with wood. That is a blessing. 57° 50' N, 42° 53' W.

Sunday • June 20, 1880

Slight breeze from the east. The waves have significantly decreased but we make little headway, for I think that we made too great a semicircular detour, because we have followed the whole coastline at a distance of 10 to 12 miles. There the [pack] ice is wide, but it decreases towards Cape Farewell. [However], 5 to 10 miles east of Cape Farewell, some sealers were able to get within 2 miles of the coast, and [there] they saw little ice. But when we were about 15 miles eastward of the Cape, [Captain Bang] began to steer southward for several days, and only then he began to steer westward. I ask [myself] for what purpose is this great semicircle being made. I have tried a couple of times to tell him [Captain Bang] my opinion, but the Captain told me off in such a vile manner by using words which cannot be written down, that I decided that I would not have anything more to do with him. The mood of the crew is also getting bad, and in the mess cabin it is quite disagreeable. As mentioned, there is little comfort, and once the Eskimos come on board (assuming that we will get any) it will be doubly crowded. And in addition, [so far], there were just 3 or 4 [seals], of whom only half were caught, or of which we were able to only get a part. There was only one chance in 14 days to catch anything, and from here on, there will be no more opportunity to catch anything (unless we happen to encounter a Greenland whale). So certainly an injustice will be done to those people [i.e., the sealers and whalers on the ship], when they do not get anything of value. If one goes on a voyage in order to catch something, that [voyage] will last at least 2 to 4 months. And if one gets anything, it will be divided. But if one has been unlucky, and caught nothing, then, of course, everybody has to accept his fate.

Monday • June 21, 1880

Headwind from the NNE. Today, after a long time, we finally have some sunshine. That seems like a miracle to me. But in spite of this, it is cool, because the wind blows off Greenland. The sea is very calm, so that I spent several hours on the deck.

Now we are so far south, and the wind is from the north. We are headed towards central Labrador. If, however, we had passed close to Cape Farewell, then we would have avoided sailing a distance of at least 20 miles from east to west. And added to this, is the misfortune that we have nearly no more water to speak of: 1 barrel of water from Hamburg, and 1 barrel of rain water. If we had come closer to the Cape, we would have found ice, and therefore also water. We saw only one iceberg, but it was so far to the lee side that we did not plan to stop.

Tuesday • June 22, 1880

Northerly wind, slightly foggy, but the air is so dry that we are able to dry our wet sails somewhat. Towards evening, the sun appeared. There was a slight breeze from straight ahead. We maintain the ship on course, but do not advance.

Wednesday • June 23, 1880

Clear sky and slight air current from the north. There is no possibility of getting any good wind. It looks quite bad with our water supply. If we do not encounter an iceberg soon, then we will soon have to hand it out in small portions. Along the east coast of

Greenland, we had searched for ice floes to get some fresh water or ice, but there was none to be found. All of it was ice which had frozen on the surface of the sea, and that always contains salt.

At the Cape [Farewell] we saw a kind of gull. Today, I again saw 2. Their beaks were straight just like those of a wild duck, the chest whitish, and the wing tip feathers were greyish. I was not able to obtain a specimen of them. Could it be that they were Cape /illegible words/?

Thursday • June 24, 1880

The whole day there was a slight wind from the south, just [strong] enough to allow the ship to be steered. There was beautiful sunshine, which I almost might have said was warm. I stayed on deck much of the time, and everything might have finally been nearly in order again, if I had not been plagued by diarrhea for nearly a month. I have drunk all of my rhubarb[17] and stomach drops, and in between up to 5 drops of opium twice daily, but all that does not help, it is /illegible word/ from the start.

Yesterday evening, there was a big popular celebration of St. John's Day, in our home [country], when big bonfires are lit, and today is considered to be half a holiday as well. Of course, I had some grog distributed as is customary on the evening of St. John's Day. Today was the 4th day during which we were becalmed. Today, we succeeded in salvaging a piece of driftwood lumber. It was very light and must have been lying on land somewhere, because it was not waterlogged.

However, other pieces [of driftwood] which we encountered were in that state and had not been in the hands of people.

Friday • June 25, 1880

The whole day there was no wind, and a cloud-covered sky. It is very sad.

We are lying here so far south in this [Davis] Strait (58° 17' N, 52° 53' W). There is no [drinking] water, and that far south no icebergs will appear. We literally have no luck at all.

Saturday • June 26, 1880

No wind the whole day. I have hardly ever seen anything like this; it is as if we were bewitched. Month after month has passed [during which we have encountered] either huge storms or no wind at all, and we get closer to our goal only in little goose-steps. This evening we caught a specimen of a rare cuttlefish [or octopus?]; it had 8 arms up to about 8 inches long with suckers on them, and at least 8 to 10 which had been completely lost. I kept it in order to put it into alcohol. Last night we killed three so-called storm petrels, because every night they swarm around us. They occur in great numbers in the Atlantic Ocean.

Sunday • June 27, 1880

This morning, at about 8 o'clock, we had a small breeze from the south, and a cloud-covered sky. Towards evening, the breeze turned towards the SSE. As usual in this area, we saw fin whales. That kind cannot catch other animals as food. The reason why nobody seems to bother catching them is that this kind of whale cannot be caught with ordinary harpoons and lines because it is much too strong and very lean, and half of its fat consists of stearin [candle wax], and there is almost no baleen. It is thought to be alright only in Wadsö[18] where they know how to make use of the stearin for animal food, and the meat is made into guano. Anyway, whalers usually leave this kind of whale alone. Our ship has passed several of them every day, but as often as we tried killing one, we never succeeded in hitting one with a shot.

On margin:[19]
In the Davis Strait there are some birds and kinds of fish which also occur to the east of Iceland and the Faroe Islands, especially the large predatory gulls and several kinds of petrels, and the Greenland sea horse, morse, or Mallemut.

They are as common in the Davis Strait as they are near Spitsbergen[20] and near Novaya Zemlya.[21] I have never seen the ivory seagull there.

Today, all kinds of whales are shot with the new harpoon guns using explosive projectiles, which kill right away. Much of the meat is made into fertilizer, in short, everything is being used.

Monday • June 28, 1880

Southerly breeze partly with thick fog. We passed a large iceberg. But we took no time to cut off ice. We still have rainwater, which is not so bad, and the further we get into the straits, the more icebergs — my [initial] plan is to head up the west coast for the so-called Cumberland Fjord [Sound], so that I gain at least certainty whether heathen Eskimos come along — and see how things are there. Towards evening, it grew quiet, with thick fog. 60° 36' N, 52° 31' W.

Tuesday • June 29, 1880

Quiet until 9 o'clock in the morning, then we got a breeze from SSW. Around noon the fog lifted, but by 2 o'clock, one could not even see 10 fathoms[22] away from the ship. Towards evening, it had turned into a nice breeze. I feel much better now, hoping to gain an appetite, [and] then I will soon be restored, as I have become terribly skinny.

Wednesday • June 30, 1880

SE wind with much rain. At noon, the wind turned easterly. Fresh *küling* (breeze). In the afternoon, it went northerly to NNW. Went towards east at 9 o'clock [in the] evening, it has been an uncomfortable day *and* very wet, but it is the last of June. How will July turn out for us?

It will have to be decided in July whether we will [be able to] enter Cumberland Fjord and whether Eskimos can be obtained from there, because in Greenland I fear to obtain to be able to accomplish little, because the inspector [Theodore Krarup Smith] forbids me to take along Eskimos. What should I do then?

Thursday • July 1, 1880

Today, westerly wind with fog—at 1 o'clock, visibility improved a little and a great number of icebergs appeared from 50 to 200 feet above water. We thought it was just one such collection of icebergs that had run aground, but it soon became evident that this was the solid, so-called 'western ice,' which we had met here, and we had just steered into a deepening or a bay, and since it was impossible now to make an attempt to break through, we now steered out again, which took a considerable amount of time, despite the fresh breeze from WSW. In the evening, we had come out again, and steered along the edge of the ice, because it had now become a little more visible. At noon, we were at 63° 7' N, 59° 20' W, roughly about 36–38 miles from the entrance to Cumberland Fjord, and already [we] met such mighty ^{masses of ice}. Now I am afraid that perhaps we may not get in at all. Our plan is now to go up rather high and then make a serious attempt to dare to get through. Once we reach the coast, we think we will get south more easily along the coast with the currents. It is just this malicious fog, because with the fog we cannot, of course, make an attempt to get through, even if the wind is favourable, but when is there a day here without fog?

> *On margin:*
> *The Scottish whalers used to anchor frequently in the fjords and bays of Baffinland, and met Eskimos there who often come from the south (from Frobisher Bay [now Iqaluit]) in the summer, moving north. The Americans used to (whalers) preferably stay in Frobisher Bay, and from there repeatedly Eskimo [some] travelled along to New York. In the 60s some have also been in England.*

Friday • July 2, 1880

SW wind. Fog. We had to steer towards SE all morning to get [out of] the ice, only after noon did we get out of the belt of ice and could steer a little more easterly. The so-called 'western ice' now extends right up to the middle of the strait. So there are terribly few prospects now to get across or through—the blocks of ice are too big and high. If a boat gets in between (between two ice[berg]s), it is irretrievably lost, or if you get too close to one, and it either capsizes or falls down upon the ship, it was lost, and often big chunks drop from such colossi, big enough to crush a small boat—, by comparison, the so-called shoal ice is nothing. Shortly after the time we had gradually cleared the ice, at 3 o'clock, the fog became so thick that we could not [even] see ten fathoms from the ship, [and] that means a sharp eye on the lookout, because if a ship runs in full speed against such a colossus of ice, it is [all] over. Tonight, a little better, but still fog. The wind is now southerly.

Saturday • July 3, 1880

Slack breeze from SW. At 6 o'clock, we saw the west coast of Greenland, the 'western ice' extends about 8 miles from Greenland's west coast—so it must now be about 30 miles wide. At the moment there is no hope to reach the west coast anywhere, and we therefore take advantage of the favourable wind, have therefore set a course for Jakobshavn[23] or Disko Bay respectively. I think like this; however, while we are forced to remain inactive here at the edge of the ice because there is no coming [through] penetration possible, we may [as well] conduct our business in Greenland. Then, I may as well hire Greenlanders [as] kayakers. [And] the governor can certainly not deny us what we need: one as an interpreter, and one to travel in advance with his kayak to find the settlements of the savage Eskimos for us. In brief, the Greenlanders can be very useful to us, if we reach the coast later, because in the autumn the ice usually drifts away. The reason why the ice is packed so densely this year is probably because the southern wind was predominant and blocked the ice from leaving Davis Strait, because it seems not to have left come out one bit. Fog permanently, so that we have not taken our bearings for a long time.

> *On margin:*
> *If we had known that the ice would not allow us any passage to the Cumberland coast (Baffinland), we would have done better to steer for Labrador and then along the coast to make an attempt [to go] north*

across the mouth of the Hudson Strait. Maybe we could have reached Frobisher Bay that way.

Sunday • July 4, 1880

Strong wind from SW, we are making fast progress. At noon, we received the sun. It became evident that we were almost 1 degree further north than calculated and were 15 miles west of Disko Island. From noon on we headed for Disko Bay, but the wind soon changed towards SE, exactly against [our course]. At 8 o'clock at night, we saw Disko despite the strong rain, there now blew a strong wind with much rain. We steered towards Disko Island.

About 8 o'clock, we saw Disko through the fog. We were now about 4 miles from Godhavn.[24] We cruised through the night.

Monday • July 5, 1880

Weak, varying, partly southern. Passed Godhavn at 8 o'clock in the morning. In the evening, a slack NE breeze. The fjord is tightly packed with icebergs, some of colossal size and circumference. Some of them capsize, or large chunks fall down with great noise.

---

[1] Henny was a nickname for Henriette Dorothea Christiane Kühne, Jacob Martin Jacobsen's second wife.

[2] The toll levied on cargoes ascending the Elbe River and passing the mouth of the Schwinge River was known as the Brunshausen dues.

[3] Jacobsen recorded the cardinal directions in a variety of ways. For ease of reading, we have standardized them and are using the abbreviated form. NW represents north-west.

[4] Now known as Baffin Island.

[5] Jacobsen recorded the geographical positions in a variety of ways in his journal. For ease of reading, we have standardized them. Represents the position 57° 47' latitude North, 1° 17' longitude West of Greenwich.

[6] Equivalent to about 150 to 180 metres.

⁷ Opinions differ as to which glacier Jacobsen is referring to. Could it be *Eyjafjallajökull* (Island Mountain Glacier), in the south west of Iceland world-famous for its 2010 eruption, *Snæfellsjökull* (Snow Mountain) in the most western part of Iceland, or *Vatnajökull* (Water Glacier), in the south east of Iceland?

⁸ A Norwegian word for quite a strong wind.

⁹ An anti-malarial drug.

¹⁰ A volcanic island in the Arctic located 1 000 km west of the Norwegian North Cape. Now spelled Jan Mayen.

¹¹ Now Oslo.

¹² Johann Friedrich Gustav Umlauff (1833–1889) was a prominent Hamburg merchant specializing in natural history specimen and ethnographic artifacts. His business operated from 1868 to 1974. Umlauff was the brother-in-law of Carl Hagenbeck.

¹³ Fast ice is sea ice that is 'fastened' to the coastline, to the sea floor along shoals, or to grounded icebergs. (Wikipedia)

¹⁴ Now Tasiilaq.

¹⁵ That is the same position as on the day before, although the strong East Greenland current runs southward, and it might have carried the ship somewhat southward even with light contrary winds.

¹⁶ The southernmost point of Greenland.

¹⁷ Rhubarb was one of the first Chinese medicines to be imported to the West from China.

¹⁸ Wadsö is a town in the Varangerfjord in Norway near the North Cape.

¹⁹ The handwriting is partly faint and hard to read.

²⁰ Spitsbergen is the largest island of the Svalbard archipelago.

²¹ An archipelago in the Barents Sea in Northern Russia.

²² A unit of length equal to six feet (approximately 1.8288 m).

²³ Is known today as Ilulissat.

²⁴ Known today as Qeqertarsuaq.

Recruiting in Jakobshavn

Tuesday • July 6, 1880

Small easterly breeze, at 4 o'clock in the morning, we saw a brig steering in the same direction as we. It is probably one of the Royal Danish Trading vessels, probably also destined for Jakobshavn. At 3 o'clock in the afternoon, the first Eskimo in a kayak appeared. I called out to him in Greenlandish; he knew me again and came on board, because he was from Jakobshavn. He told us all the news about the colony. Soon, a ship appeared approaching from the colony. It was my old acquaintance Carl Fleischer, who was visiting the colony—he was supposed to be transferred to /Al(m)nak/—as an assistant, and he was now waiting for the ship that was supposed to take him over there. Right after[wards] came Dr. von Haven[1] with the colonial administrator/merchant Möller.[2] It was a great pleasure to both me and them to meet old acquaintances. It was totally quiet, and the ice was not so dense, [and] I let the captain steer in the ship together with the crew and a few Eskimos, and went on shore with Mr. von Haven.

On margin:
I've reported about Dr. von Haven before. I stayed with him in the summer of 1877, when I got the first Eskimos from there. In the summer of 1877 I had travelled to Greenland with Möller's brother as

a travelling companion. So those we met here were all good acquaintances.

Fig. 22 Celebration on the *Eisbär*.
(Illustration by M. Hoffmann, 1880)

Wednesday • July 7, 1880

The ship was now anchored and secured, and at 5 o'clock in the morning, the 2nd ship came into the harbour. It was *Konstanz* from Copenhagen, the first ship for Jakobshavn this year, another one will come later. The ship was besieged by Eskimos from morning until evening; everybody from Jakobshavn knew me, of course, and wanted to welcome me, many to get schnapps. Okabak[3] and family, Kokkik was now married, Kujanje (Hendrik) had moved north to Rittenbenck [Ritenbenk] and married there. I sent a letter ^{with a kayaker} to the inspector ^{who was still living in Godhavn} and asked him for permission to buy the items ^{we needed}, for example kayaks, dogs, clothing, etc. The letter went off with a kayaker.

Thursday • July 8, 1880

Was invited to the Möller's for lunch, spent the day visiting. I brought along no money, but the merchant will lend me some to buy the necessary items.

Friday • July 9, 1880

I began buying a few items. This year you cannot get much in the colony, because the Eskimos have used up all their things, such as furs, etc. ^(especially those used for clothing, boats, and tents).

> On margin:
> I've probably reported in my book that the Eskimos who had returned from Europe did not go seal hunting for as long as their money lasted.

Saturday • July 10, 1880

Today, I bought a whole lot of /angmaset/ ^{dried stint} for dog food. /Angmaset/ is a small fish which is dried and which is abundant around Greenland, ^{northern} Norway, Spitsbergen, and Labrador, which is very popular as food with the Eskimos everywhere, ^{for people as well as for dogs during the winter}.

Sunday • July 11, 1880

Today, there was a Danish service in the church. Our crew, as well as that of the Danish ship, were all there. For lunch we were at Mr. Möller's. Afterwards, the captain of the Danish vessel with the helmsmen paid us a visit. ^{We were on very friendly terms with everybody here.}

Fig. 23 Zion church and doctor's house. Jakobshavn. ca 1900.
(Photo by Thomas Neergaard Krabbe. Wikimedia Commons)

Monday • July 12, 1880

Left for a small Eskimo village which lies 2 miles from here in a northerly direction. There, we obtained dried meat for dog food, selected a tent for myself, and ordered kamikker ^{Eskimo boots of sealskin}, which are very hard to get. Returned 11 o'clock in the evening. Dr. von Haven was with us as well. We also tried to catch fish, but had no particular luck.

Tuesday • July 13, 1880

Beautiful weather today. Was at Dr. von Haven's all day. At 6 o'clock in the evening, the Dane ^{Konstanz} sailed to the colony Rittenbenk. I have not received any mail from Godhavn; I am waiting with longing for a letter from the governor/inspector for northern Greenland.

Wednesday • July 14, 1880

Rain from morning until evening, this year there is a lot of uninterrupted rain. Southerly winds—so it seems as if the ice at the west coast will not go away at all. They say here that, as far as one knows, the coast can usually only be reached ˢᵃⁱˡᵉᵈ ᵗᵒ at the beginning of September. Have bought several small items. What I need most, ᵏᵃᵐⁱᵏᵏᵉʳ is more difficult to obtain.

Thursday • July 15, 1880

South easterly. Nice weather. Was hunting in the evening, but there were few birds. Captain Bang went fishing, which went much better. He got 24 (in Eskimo) Kaderalick (in Danish Norwegian) hellefisk.⁴ It is a kind of turbot ˢᵒˡᵉ but is (much) fatter.

Friday • July 16, 1880

Today, captain Bang went fishing again and caught more than 20 pieces of hellefisk. It is a special kind of hellefisk. It never grows heavier than 12 pounds and is very fat and delicious. I and several find it more delicious than salmon, it is grey or black on both sides and is found in deep water (between 150 and 300 fathoms). It is only to be found where there is a /Eisblink/ ᵍˡᵃᶜⁱᵉʳ nearby, and it is caught here all year round, mainly in the spring (March and April). Today, in the afternoon, Möller was on board for a visit together with his wife and sister-in-law.

Saturday • July 17, 1880

Nice weather. Northerly wind. Until now, no mail has come from Godhavn. In the evening, SW prospective rain. Was in the evening at Pastor [Christian Vilhelm] Rasmussen's.⁵ Pastor Rasmussen was married to a daughter of the late colonial inspector [Knud Geelmuyden] Fleischer from Bergen. His son Knud later became the famous explorer Knud Rasmussen (now in Copenhagen).

Sunday • July 18, 1880

Today, I received a letter from Godhavn. It sounds rather unfavourable. I am not allowed to take along Greenlanders, because the inspector's office is not allowed to concede such a thing. However, I received permission to buy 6 dogs, probably because there is a kind of dog disease here, and he knows that most of the dogs will die anyway. Furthermore, I am allowed to buy 2 kayaks and 12 pairs of kamikker (boots) and up to 6 furs. But they were not available, because I asked for them every day. It is a shame that these poor Eskimos are tyrannized in this manner, because they all wanted to come along gladly. The woman who had been in Europe cried almost daily, because she could not come along. Little Kujanje had gone to fetch his wife, he lived 9 miles from the colony, and he was fully determined to come along, but when he heard that the inspector had forbidden it, he was scared. If someone had gone along, they would have been punished.

Fig. 24 Kujanje, Kokkik, Okabak, Maggak, Ane, and Regine.
The Inuit from Jakobshavn recruited in 1877.
(Illustration published in *La Nature*, N° 233, November 19, 1877.)

On margin:
All Eskimos which I had with me in Europe in the year 1877–1878, the 4 adults [the verb is missing. Jacobsen probably meant 'received' or 'cost me'] more than 6 000 crowns, without all the other things such as tools (each a carpenter box full of tools, clocks/watches [?], some household goods and clothes). Was it therefore a wonder that they wanted so eagerly to come along again? Okabak's little daughter was dead, but he had meanwhile had another daughter (Helene).

If one, as happens so often in Europe, [especially (among)?] the Danes, holds the Eskimos to become good catchers (seal hunters), then this is not done for the sake of the Eskimos, but that the trade earns a lot, likewise all the traders get percentages ^(from the deal), so it follows, of course, that one tries everything to get the Eskimos out to hunt. It is known that the Eskimo is a slow ^(easygoing) person, and if he is not forced to do so, he does not like to go out, and *he is also* very timid, because the Danes have raised him in such a way, that as soon as he sees an angry face, he grows afraid. I have accused the Danes of having made the Eskimos into cowards, because in his hunts for seals, white whale and walrus, he proves that he possesses courage, as well as when one hears their old sagas, the Eskimo shows that in previous times ^(in earlier times) he had a wholly different courageous character. Then I often received as an answer, Yes, if he *were* not raised in this way, we could not achieve anything. As long as no reforms are introduced, the Eskimo is, and will remain to be, an adult child. One cannot deny these people the slightest intelligence because there are rather reasonable persons among them. I would almost say pleasant /?/. I know a few honourable ^(worthy of respect) exceptions. For us, there is now nothing else to do but to return without having achieved a thing. I must confess honestly that I have little hope to achieve anything in Cumberland. According to all forecasts, there is daily southerly wind in the ^(Davis) Strait, fog and rain alternate daily. I hope to sail on Tuesday if the weather permits it.

---

[1] Dr. Lambert Christian von Haven (1846–1920) was Jakobshavn's doctor from 1876 to 1881. (Source: Ilulissat Museum)

[2] Ernst Viggo Möller (1844–1891) was in charge of the Royal Greenland Trading Department store in Jakobshavn from 1878 to 1887. (Source: Ilulissat Museum)

[3] Okabak (Mikkel Kaspar Zacharias Poulsen), Kokkik (Hans Noahssen) and Kujanje (Johannes Hendrik Jensen also known as Kujagi or 'The Baron') are the Greenlanders who were recruited in 1877 by Jacobsen on behalf of Carl Hagenbeck. Okabak was accompanied by his wife Maggak (Johanne Juditte Margrethe) and their two daughters, Ane and Regine. The group was exhibited in several European cities.

[4] Greenland halibut.

[5] Christian Vilhelm Rasmussen (1846–1918) was a pastor in Jakobshavn from 1873 to 1895. (Source: Ilulissat Museum)

Departure from Jakobshavn

Monday • July 19, 1880

Departed for Rötebai[1] [Rodebay] to fetch a little dog food. Departed at 9 o'clock and arrived at Rötebai at 12 o'clock; a fresh breeze blew from SW (good wind). I bought one used tent, some pairs of boots. Returned again in the evening at 9 o'clock. Quiet and fog.

On margin:
The Greenlander Johan Reimers and his family members report about this.

Tuesday • July 20, 1880

Did the last purchase. The laws existing here ~~for the people~~ are rather ridiculous. The colony has just been provided with bread. Therefore, I thought it could be arranged to get a barrel of bread, but it was not allowed to happen. Supposedly, it is against the laws. A foreign vessel may not be provided or even helped with provisions and suchlike, because everything within the colony is meant for the Eskimos.

Wednesday • July 21, 1880

Said farewell to the European families. Wanted to sail away after lunch, but it was so quiet that we waited until 6 o'clock in the evening, lifted our anchor, and had us be conducted out, partly by Eskimos, partly by our own crew: it was totally quiet. Dr. von Haven, colonial [store] owner Möller, assistants Knudsen and Junker followed us far out. Now as the previous time I was received rather friendly by the Danes here in Jakobshavn.

> *On margin:*
> *Without difference both my crew and I were received so splendidly as probably nowhere else in the world. The cook of our ship had even absconded and wanted to stay here.*

Thursday • July 22, 1880

Slight breeze from east, partly quiet, progress is only slow. The dogs give us a lot to do.

Friday • July 23, 1880

Easterly wind. Around noon we passed Dog Island [Kitsissuarsuit]. Two kayakers came on board, who had cod. We got the fish and gave the Eskimos coffee for it. It [they?] were probably no sea[farers?], but one could notice at once that these people ᵃʳᵉ ᵐᵒʳᵉ ᶠᵃᵐⁱˡⁱᵃʳ ʷⁱᵗʰ and much better with kayaks than those of Jakobshavn. (Near Godhavn the waves are often stronger than in Jakobshavn, where they are rare.)

---

[1] Rodebay, a small community located about 15 kilometres north of Jakobshavn. Now named Oqaatsut.

Voyage to Cumberland Sound

Saturday • July 24, 1880

Still, partly negligible blowing from NE, fully clear with sunshine. I have been unwell the whole day, had a colossal headache. I never felt unwell so often aboard a ship. Nowhere have I encountered more worries (than here) since the first day that I set foot on this ship. On my first voyage to Spitsbergen as captain ^{of my father's ship *Elida*}, only 10 years ago (1870), I had more luck, everything went as wished for. Now, however, all my courage will soon be gone, my prospects on the return are misery and want.

Sunday • July 25, 1880

SE wind with fog, partly rain. In the evening, we met already a few pieces of ice. We tried to fish on a bank between 16 and 45 fathoms, but did not catch a single fish. There were supposed to be a lot of cod and hellefisk[1] ^{halibut} at this time. Have also caught some here a few years ago. It was, however, later in the year.

Monday • July 26, 1880

Have kept crossing because the rain and fog allow us no sight across the ice. Wind SW. Saw flat ice shoals in the evening, but do not know how many.

Tuesday • July 27, 1880

Strong breeze from SW with increasing waves. We took down the sails and kept her steadily cruising, but have not seen any massive ice until now, only single pieces. I am still unwell; it is probably from the food here, I seem no longer able to digest the food on board.

Wednesday • July 28, 1880

Wind SW, decreasing. High waves, strong rain, alternating with fog. Got quiet in the evening with thicker fog and high waves.

Thursday • July 29, 1880

Slack. SW breeze. Afternoon, NW with fog. It was so cold that all the ropes were ice-covered. Towards 6 o'clock in the evening, it cleared up. We were at the edge of ice, surrounded by masses of small ice, steering along edge towards the west.

Friday • July 30, 1880

SE with rain. Steered among small ice towards west. In the evening, we were forced to lay by. It was also fog and additionally rain. Bad prospects.

Saturday • July 31, 1880

Easterly wind, foggy. Tried to penetrate through the thick, fast packed ice, but it was lying so tightly together that penetration is impossible with our ship. It grew a bit lighter, and as far as the eye could see there was ice and nothing else but ice. Only in the east there was open sea (from where we came). It is still 15 to 20 miles up to the coast. There is little hope to get through. Searched for open sea again to make an attempt towards the south [out of] the ice chamber. Thick fog again. (Isn't there ever a day here without rain or fog?) Three years ago the weather here was totally different. There were daily partially clear northern skies with [4] to 17° + R. That was in Jakobshavn. This year, however, is totally different. Now comes the month of August. What is it likely to bring?

Sunday • August 1, 1880

Cleared up at 4 o'clock in the morning. Sailed along the ice edge. Towards noon, we began to break through the ice. The wind was NE. It was also a good view. It went quite well. The ice was so spread out that we were advancing at racing speed. At noon, we were 17 miles from the coast. At 8 o'clock in the evening, the fog suddenly began again and we were forced to stop our progress. We had penetrated into the ice up to 7 miles, so we had the hope to reach the coast. But it was meant to be different, because bad luck seems ^{to follow us}. It will not give up on us.

Monday • August 2, 1880

Thick fog until 11 o'clock in the morning. Then, it cleared up a little. Unfortunately, it revealed so much and such tightly packed ice that all penetration to the land had to be given up. I suggested we should bear west along the [coast] ^{towards south}, but the captain [Bang] was of the opinion that there was nothing else to do but get out of the ice in the same direction and then try again further south. The ship was turned south to get out ^{of the ice}. All afternoon we drifted and sailed among ice, because it had grown foggy again. It has turned into a fresh breeze and the last two days were so cold that all the ropes are full of ice; the water freezes on deck.

Thus, our high hopes were thwarted again. I have no high hopes either to reach land; the ice conditions are too difficult. All my courage is gone. Ruin remains the only prospect on returning home.

Tuesday • August 3, 1880

Storm and rain from SE. Keeping her crossing between ice floats. We cannot have been far from the open sea, because heavy waves are rolling towards us. It was a dangerous manoeuvering between so much ice in such a storm, and with so much rain that one could hardly see a cable's length from the ship. The nights are also beginning to grow dark. We saw ourselves forced, therefore, to steer the ship deeper into the ice to get to calmer waters at least. This succeeded very well, and soon we had so much ice around us that we could not notice any sea.

Wednesday • August 4, 1880

Fog and easterly wind. The storm has given up, keeping her crossing between the ices. At noon, we stood against the sea, but it began clearing up towards the evening, and we turned towards the land again. In most cases, the ice here is spread so far apart that one can get through quite well. If only it were so all the way to the land! One believed to have seen land from the lookout at 8 o'clock, but it was probably an error, and even if it was land, it could be at least 10 miles off, and the ice reflections show us that there is still a lot of ice between us and the land. At 9 o'clock, it began growing foggy again, and again we could not advance. This constant rain and fog really cause despair. We cannot even dry our clothes. Since our departure we have not had eight days without rain or fog.

[1] Cf. July 15 and 16. Jacobsen gives a different German translation of the word 'hellefisk.'

Voyage in Davis Strait

Thursday • August 5, 1880

Advanced up to 5 miles from the coast but had to turn back at 3 o'clock in the morning. It was tight with small ice floats, and it became so foggy, that nothing was visible but ice. The captain [Bang] also seems to be too fearful, because his solution seems to be that as soon as ice is seen to turn around, and what can I do about it? He has the authority on board. So, it was turned around again, and we sailed about 18 nautical miles before we came clear of the ice. What to do now? From Cape Walers[1] to Leopold Island we have tried to reach the coast. Further south on Cumberland there is no hope to reach the coast. I have made the decision to steer south towards Labrador and make an attempt to reach the coast. In these dark nights and fog there are, unfortunately, too many disadvantages to our enterprise, and we will meet masses of ice even there, but an attempt has to be made because it will take a long time until the ice becomes so thin to allow passage for our ship. Wind casterly with fog. Partly rain.

Friday • August 6, 1880

Easterly wind. [Thick] fog. We steer towards the SW. We are now completely out of the ice. There are no pieces to be seen. For more than eight days, we have not been able to take an observation, therefore our ship's position is not determined. It is practically impossible to take a reliable position because the course is constantly changing because of the ice.

Saturday • August 7, 1880

Easterly wind, weak breeze with fog. In the evening, the wind turned north east, visibility improved slightly. We are fast proceeding south, and there is a marked change in climate. While during the last eight days we had continual frost and partly snow, the weather has now turned milder. Probably because we have come out of the icy region.

Sunday • August 8, 1880

Northerly wind. From noon we began steering towards the coast; about 4 o'clock, we already saw many large icebergs. The wind, unfortunately, went NW, so we made little advance. At noon, we took a kind of observation, not a complete one, but we saw that the current had taken us far south. The current runs towards the south with great speed as one can see it virtually on the water. Thick clouds in the evening, it will probably rain again.

Monday • August 9, 1880

Wind NNW, thickly clouded. At 4 o'clock in the morning, we could see the coast of Labrador. We steered NW towards land, but towards noon, it became totally calm. We took observation. It showed that the island towards which we were steering our course was Watchman Island. According to our map, it was situated directly across from the mission station Hebron, with a good harbour that we thought to enter. There are a number of large icebergs drifting around here, but no pack ice is visible.

At 4 o'clock in the afternoon, breeze from SW, it lasted only until 8 o'clock, and then it grew still again. We were to the north of the island. Clouded sky.

Fig. 25 Iceberg, Labrador coast.
(Painting by Arthur Philemon Coleman, [1915]. Victoria University Library (Toronto))

---

[1] Would Cape Walers actually be the Cape Prince of Wales located on the Ungava Peninsula near the village of Kangiqsujuaq (61° 37' 0" N, 71° 30' 0" W)? As for Leopold Island, it is located near Cumberland Sound (64° 58' 0" N, 63° 23' 0" W). (Canadian Geographical Names Database)

ARRIVAL IN LABRADOR

Tuesday • August 10, 1880

Fig. 26 Hebron from the hills.
(Painting by Arthur Philemon Coleman, [1915]. Victoria University Library (Toronto))

Still until 11 o'clock in the morning. After 11 o'clock, a fresh breeze from south. In the afternoon, easterly. Steered towards the harbour of Hebron. Evening fresh breeze from NE. Entered the harbour and anchored in the evening at 7 o'clock. In the harbour lies one sloop, the *Wilke* which was on a voyage to ^the mission station^ in Ramah. They brought the missionary, Schneider [Johann Georg], who is now employed at Ramah. I went on shore. Made the acquaintance of the above-named gentleman, also of the gentlemen Krismer[1] [Kretschmer] and Hauch [Haugk], who are settled here, all belonging to the ~~Brüdter~~ Brüdergemeind[sic]e [the Moravian Brethren]. They possess the coast from Hopedale to Ramah ^(that means their mission territory is from Hopedale to Ramah). They also conduct the trade with the indigenous people ^(to cover some of the expenses for their missionary enterprise). The number of those belonging to the mission stations, ^(namely the Eskimos), is supposed to run up to 1500 people. There are six mission stations. Their names are [from] southernmost: Hopedale, then Zoar, Nain, where the leadership resides, then further north comes Okak, ^(Okak means cod), Hebron and northernmost lies Ramah. The missionaries here do not seem to want to further my enterprise, as I had hoped. When I told them that I had brought Eskimos from Greenland to Europe, they all insisted that the people must have been spoiled for life, because taking a trip to Europe appears to be the same as ruining ~~the souls~~ of these people ^((Unfortunately, they were to be proven right, as we will see)).

> *On margin:*
> *The missionaries in Labrador belong to the Moravian congregation in Saxony. The same people also have two stations in South Greenland (Friedrichsdal [Friedrichsthal] and Lichtenfeld [Lichtenfels]).[2] All products which the Eskimos catch, furs, skins, fish and oil,[3] are bought by the missionaries against European trade goods, which the missionaries themselves buy in England, and which are brought from there by English vessels. The ships then take the traded goods to England.*

Wednesday • August 11, 1880

The missionaries and their ladies were on board for a short visit. I was also invited for lunch. I got to know that very close by there are some old graves and, together with two of my crew members, I paid them a visit. They were old graves from pagan times, and I received explanations for a lot of things I did not know. Next to each grave, and partly also inside of it, the things are buried ^(laid) down, occasionally also inside the grave which had belonged to the deceased. It seems, however, that the items were broken before, because all containers were broken apart, even in places that were otherwise entirely secure. It is the custom among the Eskimos, that an item which belonged to a deceased, will never be used by others. Therefore, everything is carried to the grave and deposited on top of it. There, one finds remnants of kayaks, tents, omiaks (larger boats), and household items; in short, all the possessions left behind by an Eskimo. One could therefore still gather a rich collection in Labrador, if one has time to search, because the missionaries do not care about it. It is different in Greenland, where everything has been searched through by Europeans. I was quite surprised that all implements were made of wood and iron, only few of bone or stone. Indeed, I only found one spearhead of stone, and only a few insignificant implements of bone.

Fig. 27 Eskimo grave in Labrador.
(Painting by Arthur Philemon Coleman, ca 1915. Victoria University Library (Toronto))

On margin:
I had examined the graves at various places in Labrador and taken along everything suitable for a museum. Since the oil lamps there, as

in Greenland, are mostly made of soapstone, they were hence not broken so easily. Therefore, I found several still in good condition, which, of course, I took along as well. Since, as one will see later, the tragedy hit us mainly in Paris, so the collection stayed there as well, and later in the museum there (Trocadero).

Everything quite rotten (decayed), although wood keeps longer in a cold climate, it signifies a significant age, and in several graves, there was no trace of ^(human) bone remnants. Many objects of European origin were found. In each second grave there were iron nails, stemming from boat planks, and often iron pots, one bucket, and in two graves I also found pearl necklaces also from Europe, brass buttons, and stained glass framed in brass and even a thimble of brass, all of this in graves that were more than two hundred years old, because there were no traces of ^(human) bones to be seen anymore. In one grave, I found one of the small wooden puppets, which are frequently found in graves in Greenland. An Englishman, ^(who) had stayed here a long time, said that these are carried by the wild Eskimos as pagan idols, also as amulets on the arm. The bows were all so rotten, that none were to be taken along, not [even] one piece. Likewise, the arrows, but I kept three pieces of three different arrows; all had iron points made from nails. In several graves, there were also small stones, rounded, very weighty, of a kind of stone that I do not know. I also found a heavy iron stone. Should this perhaps be a meteor stone? I also found stones to whet their knives, as well as fishing gear, /Wicheln/ made of wood, wooden rolls, fishing hooks, mostly of iron, also of bone and iron. I only found few harpoons of bone and iron. Modern ones mounted on wood, as used these days, I found in almost every grave, or in the vicinity ^(of the grave).

Fig. 28 Collecting in Hebron graves.
(Illustration by M. Hoffmann, 1880)

In earlier times, the Eskimos buried their dead under steep cliffs, most popularly in front of moraines, and where many rocks have slid down from the cliffs. The graves were [made] of rocks, mostly next to a larger rock, and as many rocks as possible heaped on top. There are supposed to be many graves on the outermost islands, [and] a lot of things made of bones are buried ^{or are inside a grave}.

> *On margin:*
> *Since I took along everything that was somewhat suitable for a museum, and since later the black pox [smallpox] broke out among our Eskimos, I have sometimes pondered whether this terrible disease could have originated from one of the graves or from the items taken, because we do not know of having been in a city where the black pox raged, unless it could have been in Prague.*

> *In the end, I had brought together quite a quantity of antiquities (grave finds), and what surprised me somewhat was that none of the Eskimos living there seemed to have anything against it, because I heard no opposition from their side.*

Thursday • August 12, 1880

Today, captain Bang and three of our crew and an Eskimo as a guide travelled to hunt caribou.⁴ [I] Talked today to several Eskimos about going to Europe. Two families seemed to me to have decided to come along if the missionaries were not opposed. I then asked those gentlemen missionaries. They said it would never work, because, first of all, they had no permission from their superiors in Germany; secondly, because of the Labrador or the Hudson's Bay Company and they then insisted firmly, that the people would be spoiled by it because the Eskimos are, ^{as they said}, a reckless people, etc. All of my counter arguments were in vain.

> *On margin:*
> *Labrador is very poor in larger game. Several years later two Englishmen undertook a trip across the peninsula from west to east. They only had as much provisions as they could carry. On their way, they ran out of provisions, and one of the travellers piteously died of hunger.⁵*

However, the Eskimos are a people who possess no independence. Whatever the Europeans living in the country tell them is the law. Therefore, the missionaries had nothing more pressing than to forbid the Eskimos the voyage, and, of course, their order was lent a better ear than my offer, because I was, after all, a foreigner. However, there is one family who would come along, in spite of the prohibition, but they cannot persuade another to come as well, and one family is just too little. I have made the proposal to him [the head of the family?], to penetrate further north with me and, if possible, to persuade the wild Eskimos to come along. But he said it would be of no avail, because the savages are spread out everywhere across the rocky mountains ^{on caribou hunts} and therefore difficult to find. They are also mistrusting ^{suspicious of foreigners}, because they are often cheated in trade with the schooners which come from Newfoundland ~~Labrador~~ to barter. Namely, the schooners go to catch cod in the month of August all along up the coast of Labrador ^{up to the north}.

> *On margin:*
> *I want to try to persuade this Eskimo [to come along] as guide and interpreter towards the north of the peninsula, because here in Labrador, the language is significantly different from Greenland. In addition, the Greenlanders do understand a few words of Danish, so that, whenever I do not know the Greenlandic word, I say it in Danish and am understood.*

Friday • August 13, 1880

Was at the old graves today, and searched for antiquities. I have to be cautious, however, that the Eskimos do not see me, because the people are superstitious, and think God knows that when I burrow through their old graves here, because I have not given up all hope yet, that I may perhaps persuade another family to leave their home to follow us despite the intrigues of the missionaries.

> *On margin:*
> *Have noticed that, after all, the Eskimos do not like to see one messing around near the graves of their ancestors, probably more because of the spirits of their ancestors.*

Saturday • August 14, 1880

Today, as always, bad weather. Cold, northerly wind and fog. In the evening, snow and rain ^{all mixed up}. Again, I spent all day trying to persuade the Eskimos to come along, promised a lot to the people, but still one is too scared to come along, because the missionaries have forbidden it. It is sad to see the people under the stick, suppressed so slavishly, and even more so, that the Europeans show their power in such a manner. If our cause were not so well recognized and honourable, but thus it is a shame, because the missionaries all know Hagenbeck by name, and I have also shown them my power of attorney, all in vain. Of modern equipment little is seen among the Eskimos, the gun has widely displaced the harpoon, which is only used for hunting walrus, less for sealing. Their summer clothing, and here among the Christians, only woollen clothes, fewer furs. The women go in skirts like our ladies. Their tents are mostly of sealskin from the saddle-seal[6] (and) are pitched differently from those in Greenland; more like the Indians do theirs. Winter houses are like in Greenland. Their kayaks are significantly bigger than those in Northern Greenland, but also made much coarser, not adorned with bones. They also have a lot of wooden boats from Newfoundland.

> *On margin:*
> *Since the missionaries mostly exchange the furs against woollen blankets, which the Hudson's Bay Company produces, with which the missionaries are connected, they [the Eskimos] and especially the women, make for themselves clothes out of the Australian wool blankets. Here, all household implements also are of European origin, so that a collector finds little of what the Eskimos otherwise have in other regions. The many bone carvings found on Greenland kayaks are totally absent here in Labrador.*

With these boats in the summer they fish trout, ᵃ ᵏⁱⁿᵈ ᵒᶠ ˢᵃˡᵐᵒⁿ, ʷʰⁱᶜʰ ᵗʰᵉ ᴱⁿᵍˡⁱˢʰ ᶜᵃˡˡ ˢᵗᵉᵉˡʰᵉᵃᵈ. There is an abundance of trout here. Cod is also caught a lot by the islands and in the fjords. All products, e.g. furs and blubber oil, are bought by the missionaries and paid significantly better than in Greenland ᵇᵉᶜᵃᵘˢᵉ ᵒᶠ ᵗʰᵉ ᵗʳᵃᵈᵉ ᵐᵒⁿᵒᵖᵒˡʸ, since there is no trade monopoly here ᵃˢ ⁱⁿ ᴳʳᵉᵉⁿˡᵃⁿᵈ, and the schooners from Newfoundland screw [turn] up the prices, but manufactured and colonial goods are also much higher here than in Greenland. In the fall a lot of seals are caught, especially when the ice settles (freezes). In spring (June, July), the Eskimos travel with their boats to the outermost points of the land and islands and catch /Robben/[7] seal mainly wal[rus], in the course of two months 1–200 seals, Greenland seals, which are also caught in many thousands by the Newfoundlanders. Autumn and spring, /theilf?/, in winter, walrus is also caught. As soon as August begins, the Eskimos go to the deep fjords to catch trout ˢᵃˡᵐᵒⁿ. Up to 20 barrels of these are caught by one family.

> *On margin:*
> *It must probably be the same kind of salmon, as they occur in the northeastern United States and the New England States, about which the first Icelanders reported, when they had settled in Massachusetts shortly after the discovery of America by Leif Ericsson.*[8] *Oddly enough, it does not seem to occur in Northern Greenland, because there I have [seen] only trout (with red flesh).*

For each barrel 1 £ 20 s. is paid, and it is sold again in Newfoundland. The Greenlanders are markedly better sealers than those [the Eskimos] in Labrador, also more lively, but that is because of the local missionaries would call them reckless if they showed as much joie-de-vivre as the Greenlanders. In their intellectual capacities, those here may be a little better than the Greenlanders, because in the winter they all go to the colony, whereas the Greenlanders live more scattered. The children must also go to school daily in the winter.

> *On margin:*
> *Also, I nowhere saw a kayak with a harpoon rack, a harpoon with a line, or a float for the catch (Avertak). They seem therefore to hardly*

catch seals in the open sea, because otherwise they would, of course, have to use a harpoon, because the seal sinks down as soon as it is hit.

Tonight, our people came back, but had no luck. Two caribous had been spotted, but they got none. Today, it snowed and rained all afternoon. Northerly wind.

Sunday • August 15, 1880

Today, I recruited as an interpreter the man who was inclined to come along to Europe. It was not possible, however, to take along the woman and children as well. I intend, however, to sail off today or tomorrow and to make a last attempt to visit Nachvak, a little Eskimo village in a fjord to the north that is inhabited by pagans. There, however, is an Englishman, i.e. Newfoundlander, employed by the ~~Bafins~~ Hudson's Bay Company to trade wares with the indigenes; but the people there are pagan. Now it is difficult to find the people, because they are on the caribou hunt up in the mountains. But I have to make an attempt even if I have little hope to succeed. It is difficult with such timid people, as the Eskimos are, to persuade people to embark on such a long journey. I have, unfortunately, had the experience [that] without a direct order from Europe, neither the Danes in Greenland, nor the German missionaries here, will give me the least support. On the contrary, the poor Eskimos are intimidated to such an extent that it is impossible to get someone to come along.

Bought a kayak today and made everything ready for the voyage. It was still all day.

On margin:
The man who agreed to go north with me as an interpreter was called Abraham and was a baptized and rather intelligent man, with whom

I could communicate tolerably well, because he was used to dealing with Europeans.

Monday • August 16, 1880

Raised the anchor at 7 o'clock. Wind northerly. At the same time, a ship went out with a mission official for Ramah. It soon grew quiet, and in the evening, we had to drop our anchor, because the current went south, and there was thick fog as well. We were in close vicinity of the harbour of Hebron, at the entrance (mouth).

Our Eskimo interpreter is one of the most intelligent Eskimos I have met so far. He possesses a lot of knowledge, he writes a good hand, plays organ, violin ^(fiddle), guitar, knows most countries and larger cities, speaks a bit of English, is a good sealer, dog sledder, etc.

On margin:
The difference between high and low tide is reported to be up to 60 feet. A ship that casts anchor at 15 fathoms at high tide may risk running aground at low tide.

Tuesday • August 17, 1880

NW breeze. Around noon, we were passed by the sloop and a bark [?], both headed for Ramah, the sloop to take the missionary there, the bark to deliver goods, provisions, etc., [and] to take oil, and furs back to London. At 8 o'clock in the evening, it grew quiet again. We are not far from the entrance to Nachvak, our destination. The current nearly always runs south, so it is difficult to come north, and often the wind is still.

On margin:
Low and high tides are exceptionally great on the coast of Labrador, as well as on the coast of Newfoundland and further south. On our map it was showing 'King tides.'

Wednesday • August 18, 1880

Quiet and a strong southerly current. Located at the fjord towards Nachvak, but drifted south again in the afternoon with the current. At 4 o'clock, we got wind from SE and rain. Steered into the fjord. The maps are totally useless here, because they are designed totally wrong, and our interpreter has never come as far north. At 12 o'clock midnight, we anchored at 8 fathoms depth. We fired several gunshots at first to see if any people were nearby. We soon saw light and received an answering shot, and since the depth was alright, we dropped our anchor. So, there must be Eskimos in the vicinity. The fjord is deep and narrow, one /Schwei?/[9] runs in southerly direction, opposite from where we are now lying at anchor. Will therefore make new attempts tomorrow, to acquire people.

---

[1] Jacobsen is referring to Brother Carl Gottlieb Kretschmer who was posted in Hebron when he visited.

[2] Friedrichsthal is a Moravian station created in 1824. It was named in honour of Frederick VI of Denmark. It is known today as Narsarmijit and is the southernmost settlement in Greenland about 50 km north of Cape Farewell. The Moravian mission station Lichtenfels was created in 1748 and is known today as Akunnat. All Moravian missions in Greenland were surrendered to the Lutheran Church of Greenland in 1900.

[3] The German word 'Tran' means both 'train oil' (whale oil) or fish oil.

[4] Here and throughout the remainder of his diary, Jacobsen actually used the word 'reindeer' instead of 'caribou.'

[5] After consultation with Philip Schubert, author of *Letters to the Granddaughter - The Story of Dillon Wallace of the Labrador Wild*, we believe that Jacobsen is referring to the 1903 expedition of Dillon Wallace, Leonidas Hubbard, and George Elson. None were

Englishmen (Wallace and Hubbard were Americans while Elson was a Canadian voyageur from the Missanabie Cree First Nation near James Bay) and they started from the east side of the Labrador Peninsula. However, their expedition did end in the death by starvation and exhaustion of the trip leader, Leonidas Hubbard. Dillon Wallace published a book in 1904, *The Lure of the Labrador Wild*, which became a bestseller and is still in print. The tragedy also triggered two competitive expeditions in 1905 across Labrador, following the route planned in 1903. One was led by Dillon Wallace, the other by Mina Hubbard, Leonidas' widow. George Elson was a member of Mina Hubbard's team. Both expeditions were also the subject of books. One of the three books above most likely ended up in Jacobsen's hands. Philip Schubert has spent the last decade retracing the various routes taken by the above explorers on their respective expeditions.

[6] Greenland seal.

[7] The German word 'Robbe' used by Jacobsen is the generic term identifying pinnipeds including seals ('Seehund') and walrus ('Walross').

[8] Since Anne Stine and Helge Ingstad's exploration of the Labrador and Newfoundland coast in 1960, we know that the 'Leifsbudir' (Leif's huts) were not in Massachusetts, but at L'Anse aux Meadows on the northern tip of Newfoundland, from where the wooded coast of Labrador (Markland) is visible on a clear day.

[9] The German word is not clearly legible, it could be a misspelled 'Zweig' (branch), indicating that a branch of the fjord opposite Nachvak runs in a southerly direction.

In Nachvak

Thursday • August 19, 1880

Went on land at 7 o'clock with my interpreter and one sailor in a direction where we saw smoke. There were four families present and we learned from these people that they are the only inhabitants of Nachvak because the others had moved inland and would only return in October. They were now hunting caribou; the meat and fat are dried and kept for the winter.

> *On margin:*
> *There were only older people who were no longer useful for a strenuous hunt like that for caribou, who were here now to catch salmon and to dry it.*

These were all older people; only the young ones go into the inner land. Because hunting is too tiring, they are left behind. They now subsist on catching trout, of which there are many here, and in exchange for tobacco and matches you can get a lot of trout. I invited the people to visit our ship, and at noon, had all four families on board. I fed them well, and after that I made them the proposal to come along to Europe. In the beginning, no one would, but my interpreter knew how to persuade the people (I had promised him a new suit if he could convince somebody to travel with us) so one family at last decided to come along. It was a man, an older woman, and their daughter. But from where will I get the others? [In the] afternoon, we prepared our biggest boat to go say hello to the European settler ^{in the colony}. I had made his brother (the captain of the ship) give me a letter of recommendation, which I delivered to him. It was stormy and rainy, southerly wind. We arrived there at 5 o'clock in the afternoon. We received a very friendly welcome. Nearby lives a young mixed one [Métis] who, together with his wife, was just visiting. A big steamship came right after us, the only ship that comes here in a whole year. It was a great delight because the ship also delivers the mail and the provisions for the whole year and only comes back here next year in August.

> *On margin:*
> *It seems therefore that in Labrador also the reindeer migrate north in the spring and south in the fall, just like everywhere in Canada, or wherever else reindeer are found. But I have already mentioned elsewhere that Labrador was really poor in reindeer.*
>
> *I soon became exceptionally good friends with the fur trader, Mr. [George] Ford. He was one of those honest characters whom you meet now and then among those who live by themselves and are seldom in touch with the outside world.*

I went with Mr. Ford on board the ship called *Labrador*, commanded by Captain [Alexander] Gray,[1] in the hope of getting some coals. But it was all in vain. In my opinion, Captain Gray is an unfriendly and arrogant man. I tried to get from him only eight tons (barrels), which for him would only last two hours, and told him also that we were in the greatest need, but he totally refused my request and was rather unfriendly all evening long.

Fig. 29 Ford's House - Last house and the North Atlantic Coast.
(Painting by Arthur Philemon Coleman, ca 1915. Victoria University Library (Toronto))

Fig. 30 Ford's House. Nachvak Bay, Northern Labrador.
(Painting by Arthur Philemon Coleman, ca 1915. Victoria University Library (Toronto))

I found Mr. Ford's house the more accommodating, where I stayed overnight. I was accompanied by one of the Eskimos to serve as a guide, in case I made an attempt to go into the interior of the country, but he did not feel like it and explained it [to be] impossible to find the Eskimos there, because it was uncertain in which direction they had gone and Mr. Ford, who was very interested in my project, said it would be almost impossible to find the people in the course of 10 days, we would be unable to take provisions for longer, our two pairs of boots (Kammik) would not last, all Eskimos north of here (of them there are only 8 to 12 families) had also gone into the interior towards the south, and to go to Ungava Bay our supply of coals would be too small. May I not call my fate an unfortunate one because, if I had come here 14 to 18 days ^{earlier}, then I would have been able to get people, because Mr. Ford would have encouraged them to it, and would probably have been able to persuade them?

> *On margin:*
> *The commander of the Hudson's Bay's steamer Labrador, Mr. Gray, as a true Brit, was probably so unapproachable and uncooperative against us because we were not Englishmen, and he, like the missionaries in Hebron, had probably regarded us as unwonted intruders. Surprisingly enough, Mr. Gray visited me in Dresden a few years later, because he had a sister [there], who was married to a German. In Dresden he was totally different towards me than in Labrador.*

Friday • August 21 [20], 1880

Southerly wind, nice weather. This morning the guide we hired here ran away. He did not feel like guiding us into the interior and has turned back with his kayak without any further ado. Mr. Ford has now talked at length to my interpreter and he obtained his promise to go to Europe with me, provided I supply his mother with provisions until he returns next year, which, of course, I promised immediately. So, we have to return to Hebron to fetch his family. I am very pleased about that and I am convinced that, despite my many efforts, I would not have succeeded in persuading him to come along without Mr. Forster's ^(Ford's) help. He speaks the language well because he is born in Labrador of English parents. In the afternoon, I was at an old burial site, also found a number of things like household utensils, etc. Returned to our ship, only Ford accompanied us on board, where we arrived at 9 o'clock at night. Mr. Ford spent the night on board. I bought various items from him, like clothes, etc. Calm and clear sky in the evening.

> *On margin:*
> *In my delight about Abraham's promise to come along to Europe with his wife and two children, Mr. Ford and I got solidly drunk. I was well equipped with wines, cognac, rum, and aquavit, and even though my captain Bang had secretly stolen a lot of it, there was still enough. I have repeatedly had the good luck to find people who helped me with all their might. In 1877, it was Fleischer [Carl] in Greenland and now, it is Mr. Ford here. Only his powers of persuasion succeeded in changing Abraham's mind.*

Saturday • August 21, 1880

Sent a boat to the station trading post with Mr. Ford and my interpreter fetched the family who had promised us to come along. Took all their belongings on board, including 4 dogs, 1 kayak, 1 old tent and diverse small things. Got back on board at 12 o'clock. The other boat had not arrived. There was also a strong breeze (oncoming). The boat came back at 11 o'clock at night.

> *On margin:*
> *Added to what we purchased in Greenland, we would be able to set up an impressive Eskimo village and present it.*

Fig. 31 The family recruited in Nachvak. October 1880.
Nuggasak, Paingu and Tigianniak.
(Photo: Jacob Martin Jacobsen. Nederlands Fotomuseum. WMR-903482)

Sunday • August 22, 1880

Lifted anchor at 8 o'clock in the morning, wind from SE and clear. Crossed out of the fjord. At 8 o'clock in the evening, it turned calm. We had arrived at the mouth of the fjord. Calm all night.

> *On margin:*
> *The coast of Labrador is one of the most dangerous to travel, especially with a sailboat.*

Monday • August 23, 1880

Calm and fog. High seas from SE. In the mouth of the fjord there are several reefs so we had to take the greatest precautions to avoid them, because the current puts the ship in the direction of the rocky reefs, and it is so foggy that one cannot see anything.

> *On margin:*
> *The sea went with great power against the reefs below, and since there was no wind, the strong current led us straight towards them.*

Tuesday • August 24, 1880

At 2 o'clock at night, I suddenly saw, from the ship's bow, that the current was driving us directly onto a reef *on which the waves crashed*. Had to drop anchor immediately and remained lying right at the reef, upon which the waves threw themselves ᶜʳᵃˢʰᵉᵈ with great power. We had to get away as soon as possible from this dangerous spot. At 5 o'clock, we managed to lift our anchor, and with our boats and the help of the current, which was now going in an easterly direction, to turn the ship sideways *past* the rocky reef. 9 o'clock breeze from north with snow and high waves from east. Afternoon, storm from north with high sea. Land in sight.

On margin:
It looked anything but beautiful. Added to that, the night was rather dark. In the morning, with a strong but favourable wind, we got clear of the land and steered south towards Hebron.

Wednesday • August 25, 1880

At 3 o'clock in the morning, [we] anchored again in Hebron. Lying at anchor there was a schooner-brig called *Cordelia*,[2] from London, belonging to the mission company, and two fishing schooners. At 7 o'clock, arrived the barque *Harmony*,[3] and the mission ship *Meta*,[4] and right afterwards, two more fishing schooners. We filled our water tanks and made ourselves ready to sail to Europe. Our guide Abraham is coming along with his wife and two children and another young man, ᵃ ʳᵉˡᵃᵗⁱᵛᵉ ᵒᶠ ᴬᵇʳᵃʰᵃᵐ, ᵀᵒᵇⁱᵃˢ, more could not be procured. We will thus be eight persons altogether. First Abraham, 35 years old, his wife Ulrika, 24 years old, a young girl, Sara, 4 years old, their 2nd child, Maria, 1½ years old, and a young man Tobias, 20 years old. They are all Christians. Also there are from Nachvak three pagans, namely Tiagrraniak ᵀⁱᵍⁱᵃⁿⁿⁱᵃᵏ ⁽ⁱᵗ ᵐᵉᵃⁿˢ ᴼˡᵈ Ᵽᵒˣ⁾, about 40 years old, his wife Paieno, 50 years old, and their daughter Noggasak ᵐᵉᵃⁿˢ 'ʸᵒᵘⁿᵍ ᶜᵃʳⁱᵇᵒᵘ,' 15 years old. At 9 o'clock in the evening, we were ready, and at 11 o'clock, our Eskimos came on board 'with gown and gear' as the saying goes, and all the Eskimos of half of Labrador came to the rendezvous; I believe, because the ship was filled with Eskimos. I had all of them be hosted well to put us in a good reputation ᵐᵉᵐᵒʳʸ among the Eskimos. Came to rest very late. Wind from NW and clear.

On margin:
The missionaries were not very pleased that Abraham, his family, and his nephew Tobias were travelling with us. I, on the other hand, was totally enraptured. It came very close for the great financial

investment we made to be wasted (the cost of the expedition had amounted to something like 30 000 marks). My feeling of honour was also at risk, as I, who had so to speak, planned and organized the whole project, should never have miscalculated so badly. Often during the summer I had been close to despair.

Fig. 32 The family from Hebron. October 1880.
Ulrike with Maria, Tobias, Abraham, and Sara.
(Photo: Jacob Martin Jacobsen. Moravian Archives, Herrnhut. FS_Labrador_Alb1-04r)

[1] Jacobsen is referring to Alexander Gray who was the captain of the *Labrador* from 1871 to 1882.

[2] The *Cordelia* belonged to the Moravian mission. This might have been its last visit to Hebron since the following year, in 1881, during a voyage to Europe, it was run down by a steamer in the River Thames.

[3] The *Harmony* was the Moravian Mission's main supply ship which visited the Labrador missions once a year and provided the vital link to Europe. It was owned and managed by the Society for the Furtherance of the Gospel (SFG), the trading arm of the Moravian Church located in London, England. Even though Jacobsen makes no mention of it, the arrival of the *Harmony* on August 25 must have generated lots of excitement in Hebron. As Susan Felsberg, a Labrador history enthusiast, explained: "It was said that the Labrador year did not run from one New Year to the next, but from the *Harmony*'s arrival until her return the following summer. Most Moravian communities face south for sun and shelter from the north, and each has a 'ship's hill', where a spotter was stationed to send signals as she was seen approaching through the coastal islands. She was met by kayaks and gunshots, the church brass band and singing, and the ship replied with her rockets. The station flag flew at full mast, to indicate that all was well after a dark winter, and no missionary staff had died in the past year. During her visit, all was frenzied activity, known as 'ship's time', with unloading of supplies, and reloading of export goods: hides, dried fish, seal oil, and eider feathers. Letters were received and answered, staff organized to leave or change stations, and children of boarding school age prepared to leave parents for long years in Europe. In August 1880, the ship was *Harmony IV*, a 251-ton barque (three masts), which made 36 Atlantic crossings from 1861 to 1897."

[4] The *Meta* was mainly used by the Labrador Moravian mission for keeping up the communication between its local mission stations.

From Labrador to Europe

Thursday • August 26, 1880

Took to our boats and lifted anchor at 7 o'clock in the morning. Wind NW. High seas from north. The Eskimos soon grew seasick; no wonder considering this high sea.

Passed Watchman Island at 2 o'clock in the afternoon. 3 o'clock quiet with high sea.

Friday • August 27, 1880

Breeze from NW until noon, after noon quiet. The Eskimos are suffering very much from seasickness and certainly regret having been persuaded to leave their beloved Labrador. It is a clear sky, and we see the coast of Labrador on the far horizon. A few huge icebergs lie scattered over the sea—hopefully the last ones this year. We have on board 9 big and 8 small dogs, so there is at times a terrible noise when they are fighting. I also have 3 kayaks from Labrador and 2 from Greenland, so that I hope to be able to offer a beautiful exhibition in Germany next winter. We can only wish for a fast crossing—because our coals are almost finished.

Fig. 33 Iceberg along the Labrador coast near Nachvak Fjord.
(Photo: France Rivet, 2016)

On margin:
You can gather from the previous that even in those days, there had been quite a bit of 'life' in Hebron. We had rented dogs and a solid sleigh on which we put our water barrels. Although there is no snow on the ground at this time of the year, but on the contrary it is partly quite sandy, the 10 to 12 dogs quite easily pulled the water barrels weighing about 250 to 300 litres.

The Eskimo girl in love in Hebron. Here I saw for the first time an Eskimo girl of 17 years who had fallen madly in love with a European. She could hardly be removed from the ship and cried tears when they had to go on land.

Saturday • August 28, 1880

Southerly wind and rain and still receiving waves from the NW ^(yet, the sea rolled from the north). There is /certainly?/ a fresh breeze further along in Davis Strait. In the evening, the wind turned easterly and died off.

Sunday • August 29, 1880

Today, NE wind, slight breeze. A little more wind in the afternoon. Since yesterday it has been raining incessantly. The Eskimos still suffer intensely from seasickness, especially the young girl (Noggasak). They take in neither food nor drink. I had rice porridge with raisins cooked for them of which they ate a little. Evening quiet again, with high sea.

Monday • August 30, 1880

Strong wind from North, we are proceeding fast. Unfortunately, the Eskimos are suffering much from seasickness. The waves strike high indeed. They are already asking how far it is still, the poor guys. Even with this beautiful wind, if it continued to blow like today, we could not be in Hamburg for another month. In the evening, we reefed two of our mainsails. Stormy from north.

> *On margin:*
> *I tried everything to solace/comfort my Eskimos. We have installed a comfortable (living) room below deck for the people. Instead of the hatch, we have fashioned a so-called 'Kashpe,' so that the people can go up or down at any time. We have also constructed a good staircase instead of the previous ladder, so they can walk well on it.*

Tuesday • August 31, 1880

Strong wind from NW. We are proceeding rather well, despite the fact that our ship does not sail well. The Eskimos are all suffering from seasickness. Hopefully it will go away soon. Masses of so-called cape doves[1] are fluttering around our ship, but it is not possible to catch them.

Wednesday • September 1, 1880

NW wind, fresh breeze, with small rainstorms. At 12 o'clock, we passed Cape Farewell (Greenland's southern tip). Up to now it went quite well. We have sailed 170 miles from Hebron to here. The Eskimos seem to be in a slightly better mood, despite the rough sea.

Thursday • September 2, 1880

Small breeze from north. High sea. Our ship is rolling so much that we were forced to reef our sails despite there being no wind. In the evening, a good breeze from NW. The Eskimos are very seasick, no wonder. The young girl (Noggasak) is suffering worst.

Friday • September 3, 1880

Small breeze from North with rain showers. Calm in the evening. At noon, we stood at 57° 15' N, 36° 46' W. It seems to be over with the good wind which we had until now. We have been rather lucky, because it is a fine distance, we have covered in the last eight days.

Saturday • September 4, 1880

Slight easterly breeze with calm sea. In the afternoon, the wind turned NE. The Eskimos are now fairly well, because it is the first day that the sea is so calm and they are not seasick. We advance but little.

Sunday • September 5, 1880

Light breeze from NE with high waves from east. There is little advance, and our ship is not one of the fast-sailing vessels. Evening quiet.

Monday • September 6, 1880

Quiet until noon. In the afternoon, a slight breeze from south. Still high sea from east. One dog died.

Tuesday • September 7, 1880

Slight southerly breeze, evening soft rain, still rough sea. There is an advance, but very little, and although we have made a bad trip, I do long for Europe, which has to be a sort of 'Heimweh' [longing for home], because it is always the same with me. I think little of Europe when I am on the journey, but as soon as I turn the nose towards home, it is not going fast enough. But this time especially, because I have been unwell all summer long.

Wednesday • September 8, 1880

^{Storm or strong} wind from southwest with rain. We are advancing fast, and if we had a fast-sailing vessel, we would soon reach the coast of Scotland. Unfortunately, that is not the case, and we must be content with what we have. Until now, the weather has been fairly favourable. We have not had any storms all summer long, and since we passed Iceland on our trip home, we have had almost always good wind. This afternoon we had several ^{Stygere dolphins or pig whales} before our bow. But they knew to keep far enough from the ship so that we could not reach any.

Thursday • September 9, 1880

Westerly until noon, afternoon southwesterly breeze with sunshine. Today, we passed the southern tip of Iceland (the 23rd degree latitude west of Greenwich). I fear that the wind turns south easterly tomorrow. (Today, delirious for the first time.)[2]

Friday • September 10, 1880

Quiet with waves from west. Clear skies. At noon, we were at 60° 0' N, 19° 33' W. I'm beginning to become sick again.

Saturday • September 11, 1880

Slight breeze from WSW, clear skies until 3 o'clock in the afternoon, from 3 o'clock onwards, rain breezes and SW winds. Since last Saturday we have sailed a total of 17° eastward, and if we cover the same distance by next Saturday, we will be at Fair Isle, Scotland's north coast.

Sunday • September 12, 1880

SW breeze in the morning. At noon, we were at 60° 10' N, 14° 44' [W]. Quiet in the afternoon. We have [passed? seen?] a ship (a three-masted ship) to the south, it is probably a cryolite[3] trader (cryolite is brought from southern Greenland/Arsuit to Philadelphia and US). Quiet all evening. Our good weather has probably ended.

Monday • September 13, 1880

Light breeze from north with a lot of rain showers. Between 6 o'clock and 9 o'clock in the evening, quiet with much rain. After

9 o'clock, NE breeze. We saw another ship today in northerly direction. The Eskimos are beginning now to exchange their seasickness for boredom, and they are forever asking whether we are not going to see land soon. They also see daily that we are fixing our position, and asked one of the sailors, who was at the helm, what there was to see in it [the sextant]. The good-for-nothing said that one could see Hamburg ^{through the octant} and how far it was. The Eskimos tried it as well, could not find out where Hamburg was located.

Tuesday • September 14, 1880

Fresh breeze from NW until noon. In the afternoon, the breeze decreased and 10 o'clock, it was wind still. Clear sky. Around noon we passed the /Grosse Bank/[4] southwest of the Faroes. We dropped the plumb [lead] but found no bottom because we were too far to the south. Today, 60° 20' N, 9° 24' W.

Wednesday • September 15, 1880

NE breeze with clear sky. Towards evening, the wind turned ENE. Today, we passed the latitude of the Faroe Islands and saw several large vessels, also small fishing boats, and all going westward.

Thursday • September 16, 1880

Breeze from SWS, clear skies. After noon the wind went SW. At **3 o'clock** we saw **Land**. It was **Fareloe**[5] (the westernmost of the Scottish Isles). Today is exactly three weeks since we set sail from Labrador. If everything continues to go as well as it has so far, then we may consider ourselves lucky. We have a sailor on board by the name of Lampe (that is precisely the one who is worth the least). He came last night and demanded a different bread, but the people get the same bread which we eat, and it is a rather good ship's bread. I told him that he was receiving the same bread which we ate. When he realized that he would get no different bread (I did not have a different one), he began to swear. I told him to leave the cabin. He did not want to do that and became even more abusive. I then got angry and threw him out. This morning, when I came on deck, I found that one kayak was cut to pieces and one pair of boots, which I had left on deck yesterday, had also disappeared. There is no doubt that this scoundrel did it in revenge—they are a nice lot, all of them, from top to bottom.

Friday • September 17, 1880

SSW wind, fresh breeze. At 8 o'clock in the morning, we passed Sumburg Head. In the afternoon, the wind turned south, we [headed] ESE. So the first greeting from the North Sea was headwind! Now, we must not complain because we have had good wind all summer long. May it not take too long to get to Hamburg, because it is beginning to be boring on board? Let us hope for better wind soon.

Saturday • September 18, 1880

Stormy from south, held easterly until noon, turned and held SW over until 6 o'clock, then the wind turned to the west, turned and steered course south. In the evening, rain and NW wind.

Sunday • September 19, 1880

Small breeze from the north with rain showers. In the afternoon, a schooner passed us, probably a Dane (to judge by his rigging); he stood in SE direction (towards Skage[r]rak). In the evening, NE breeze, variable, with rain.

Monday • September 20, 1880

Storm from North with heavy rain showers. At noon, fixed our position as 57° 30' N, 3° 8' E. A lot of ships passed us, some heading eastward, but most of them to the west. None came near enough for us to see their home port.

Tuesday • September 21, 1880

Westerly wind with minor rain showers in the morning. In the evening, the wind turned SW. Clear skies. A lot of sailboats and steamboats passed us. At 11 o'clock, we saw a 'water column' [a vortex of water] in SW direction, but it soon disappeared without causing damage. At noon, we fixed our position at 55° 28' N, 4° 58' E.

---

[1] Jacobsen used the word 'Captauben' which, according to Encyclopedia Britannica and Brockhaus, translates to 'Cape Dove.' Cape doves are found in Africa, Middle East or Madagascar. It seems unlikely that they would be found in the North Atlantic. We do not know how skilled Jacobsen was in ornithology. Did he actually see a Northern Fulmar? An Iceland Gull? An Ivory Gull?

[2] Jacobsen was suffering from intermittent fever.

[3] A rare mineral first discovered in Greenland. Used to produce aluminum.

[4] We are assuming that this is the name of a sandbank.

[5] This island is most likely Foula as per the geographical information provided by Jacobsen.

Storm Near Heligoland

Fig. 34 Tigianniak calming a storm.
(Illustration by M. Hoffmann, 1880)

Wednesday • September 22, 1880

Wind SW. Held directly to the wind, SE over. At 7 o'clock in the morning, we got Heligoland in sight, but the wind turned SSW, and we were positioned between Heligoland and Föhr. It started storming and it was likely we would run aground on the coast of Schleswig. The reason for our coming so far east was that our chronometer was not working correctly. We travelled with as much sail as possible and we succeeded in reaching Heligoland at

7 o'clock in the evening, where we dropped anchor. Right afterwards, the wind jumped to NNW. Strong wind. Decided to wait until 2 o'clock in the morning, so we would not enter the Elbe River too early. I had told the Eskimos that we were in the danger of running aground. Right afterwards, I went into the cabin, and all of a sudden, I heard a terrible screaming. I hurried on deck fast because I thought that someone had gone overboard or had been hurt some way. Here I was presented with a rather surprising spectacle. The pagan Eskimo ^Tiggieniak stood at the bow of the ship, gesticulated with his arms, and uttered one howl after the other. At first, I thought that he had suddenly turned mad. We stood all around him and did not know what to do with him. His voice sounded through the howling of the storm, like that of an unfortunate person in extreme danger of death. Then, one of the other Eskimos stepped forward and said we should leave him in peace, because he was in the process of making magic, namely for good wind. At the same time, his wife sat in her cabin and made the most wondrous gestures with her hands, but uttered no sounds. After he had finished howling his hexing formulas, he calmly went to his cabin with the prophecy that we would have good wind. A few hours later we really had good wind ^(north wind), and Tegienniak (that is his name and he is supposed to be well-known in his homeland as a great magician, an *Angakok*), insisted firmly, that it was his own doing ^(meaning that he had called the north wind). I was really highly pleased that the guy had not, ^(contrary to what we had believed), turned mad in the process, of which I had been convinced in the beginning. But after that, our sailors believed that Terrianiak was a real magician because the wind had turned so suddenly into a north wind from a SW storm.

Fig. 35 Heligoland, ca 1890-1900.
(Wikimedia Commons. USA Library of Congress. Prints and photographs.)

On margin:

I have [described] this scene with the Eskimo magician in my Norwegian book Kaptein Jacobsens Eventyrlige Farter *[Captain Jacobsen's adventurous travels], translated by Ingeborg v[on] d[er] Lippe. Bergen: Grieg, 1894. I have observed later that the professional magician does not always master magic, but that other Eskimos as well will suddenly feel called upon to act as magicians when in danger or when serious situations occur, and [they] will then conduct the same [ritual] which they may have seen from their magician earlier as children or later [and] do the same. For most of the wild peoples, of course, it depends mainly on whether they feel called upon to act as a magician at that moment.*

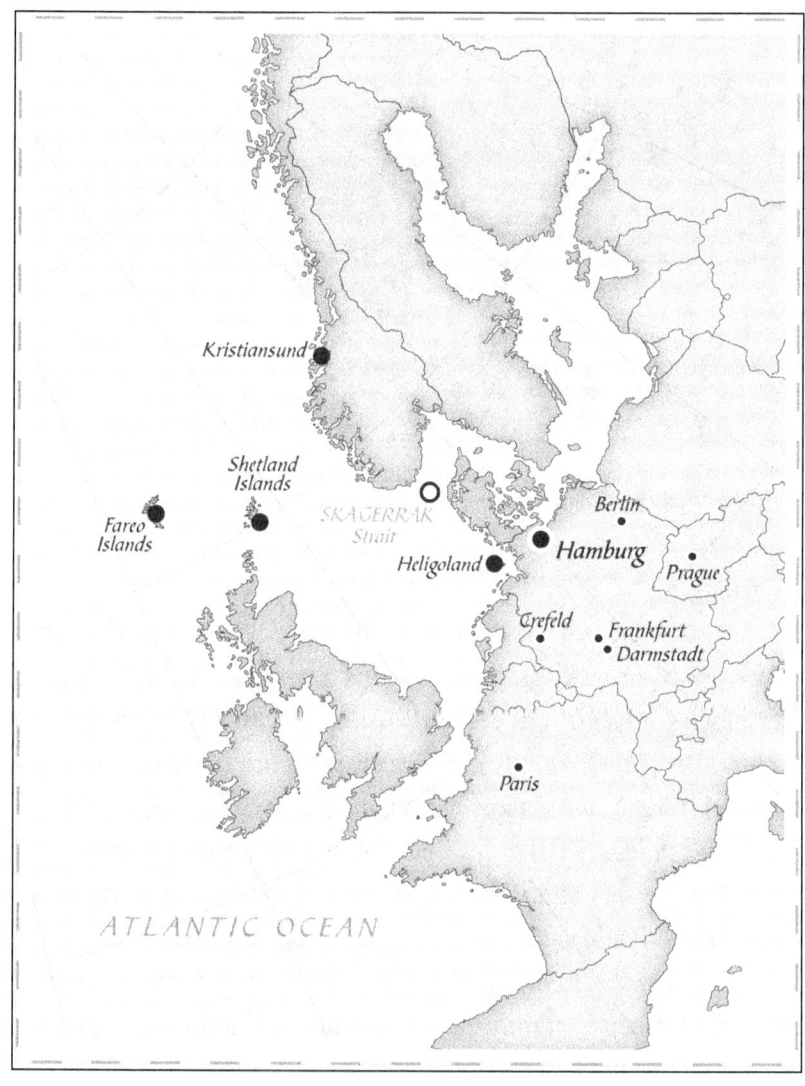

Fig. 36 Map of Jacobsen's 1880 travels in Europe.
(Illustration: Diane Mongeau)

On the Elbe and Arrival at Hamburg

Thursday • September 23, 1880

We weighed anchor, while the wind turned north, and kept her tacking[1] until 3 o'clock, because it was still too dark to enter the Elbe without a pilot. At 8 o'clock, we got a pilot at the lightship.[2] Passed Cuxhaven at 12 o'clock, and Busch at 3 o'clock, Glückstadt at 4 o'clock. I took no ~~steamer~~ towing steamer, because I was waiting for my brother, whom I had telegraphed from Cuxhaven that we were coming.

At 9 o'clock in the evening, my brother [Jacob Martin] came on board with Mr. Hagenbeck Senior and I learned, to my delight, that everything was well at home.

Friday • September 24, 1880

Arrival in Hamburg at 6 o'clock in the morning. The Eskimos and their baggage were disembarked and immediately taken to Mr. Hagenbeck brought to 13 Neuer Pferdemarkt. Mr. Hagenbeck ~~junior~~ senior was on his return trip from St. Petersburg, and I received a telegram in the afternoon to come to Berlin as fast as possible. I left for Berlin at 10 o'clock in the evening to meet Hagenbeck there.

To be inserted on page 139 of the year 1880

I want here to write down an episode from my life, which may sound somewhat unbelievable, and for which it is hard to find a match in daily life. As you can see from my diary, Carl Hagenbeck was on a journey from St. Petersburg-Berlin-Paris, when he received a telegram from Hamburg, that I had passed Kokshafen (Cuxhaven) with the Eisbär (our ship). When I arrived at Hamburg, I found a cable from Mr. Hagenbeck to immediately come to Berlin. So, I departed from Hamburg on the same evening and was in Berlin the next morning. I may well say that our meeting was mutually quite cordial, because in the 3 years during which I was at his service, we had developed a brotherly relationship. He knew that I would do my utmost to further his interests, which in this case were also my own. Because we all had equal shares in this, Hagenbeck, as well as my brother Martin and myself. Each of us (my brother and I) had invested our savings in the purchase of the ship and the equipment. During the breakfast at the hotel, I explained to him, why we did not also bring home a full cargo of sealskins and fat, as originally planned. That was due to the constant adverse wind on the outgoing voyage, and perhaps also my sickness, because if I had not been so miserable for months, I could perhaps have exhorted my people to greater activity. After all, I had been almost unconscious for days. But Hagenbeck was happy beyond all measures that I had brought the Eskimos after all, and we forged plans, where we would be able to set up our Eskimo village first and with the greatest profit. After Hamburg we wanted to start first in Berlin, where we had been so very lucky in 1878 with the Greenlanders, that Emperor Wilhelm I had looked at them. Now Hagenbeck told me the following thing. When I was [travelling] from St. Petersburg yesterday, I had a remarkable appearance just before Eydkunen. I thought I was awake but must have been fast asleep and dreaming. I felt that you had suddenly stepped into my carriage, which did not a little surprise me. I immediately asked you, have you brought Eskimos? Whereupon you replied: Yes, I am bringing eight Eskimos. At the same moment you had disappeared, and outside the window of my compartment someone called out aloud: Hagenbeck, is Mr. Hagenbeck on the train? I jumped up immediately, pulled down the window of my compartment, and called out here is Hagenbeck. Whereupon, a telegram carrier approached and brought me a telegram from Hamburg, which read: "Jacobsen just passed Kokshafen (Cuxhaven), has eight Eskimos on board." What should one say about such a dream apparition? I was very surprised, because Hagenbeck was not the man, to make such a joke, or who would be guilty of telling an untruth. What puzzled me most about the thing was that the number of people was so accurate.

We may well believe that Hagenbeck was thinking a lot about us at that period, because it was the time we were expected to return, and it could therefore easily appear in a dream, that we had finally arrived. But how come he hit on the number eight Eskimos, because my order was to bring 12 to 15 people, so that the effect would be greater with the public. In other [later] troupes, e.g. the Africans and later Indians (from India) there would always be 20 to 30 and even up to 40 people. However, these people were paid less than the Northlander Eskimos and Laplanders (Sami).

---

[1] Means zig-zaging against the wind, without gaining ground—remaining in one spot.

[2] Back in those days, pilots would wait at the 'Feuerschiff' or light (signal) ship lying at anchor before the mouth of the Elbe river. Since 1816, the lightship was positioned at about 7.5 km from the mouth of the river at the geographical coordinates 54° 0' 0" N, 8° 10' 40" known as 'Elbe 1.' In 1880, the lightship was the *Gustav-Heinrich*, a wooden three-masted schooner.

Stay in Hamburg and in Berlin

Saturday • September 25, 1880

Met Mr. Hagenbeck in Töpfers Hotel at 6 o'clock in the morning. After a cordial greeting and welcome, I drove with Mr. Hagenbeck to the zoological garden, and from there to Mr. Hoffmann (painter and author), who was hired to write a small travel account based on my diary. On our way, I told Mr. Hagenbeck most of my experiences of our journey, and then travelled <u>back</u> to Hamburg on the <u>same</u> day.

> *On margin:*
> *As always with Völkerschauen [literally: 'people's shows,' i.e. ethnographic expositions], Mr. Hagenbeck customarily employs a woman, who cooks and washes for the people. The name of this woman is Jacobs,[1] and she cares for the people like a mother. Since she has been travelling with them for years (she was also with our Greenlanders), she has received the name 'Anthropologenmutter' (anthropology mother).*

From September 26 to October 2, 1880

[We] were in Hagenbeck's garden where preparations were made to exhibit the Eskimos. Like the last time, houses were constructed (Eskimo houses), tents were pitched, the collection was set up, and we started...

Fig. 37 Tigianniak smoking pipe in his tent.
(Illustration by Adolf Liebscher. Prague's *Světozor* Newspaper. 1880-11-26.)

Saturday • October 2, 1880

... our exhibition on October 2nd. It rained and the wind blew nonstop.

Monday • October 4, 1880

Went to the K....s [Krankenhaus = hospital]. Was sick for a long time, and tried to recover through rest and medication. In the meantime, my old travelling companion, Adolph Schoepf from Dresden, had travelled to the Berlin garden with the people.

Wednesday • October 27, 1880

Travelled to Berlin *(as well)*, where the Eskimos had been already since the 12th *of October*. I met all my old acquaintances again in Berlin. My sickness had subsided, especially the unbearable headaches and diarrhea.

Sunday • November 7, 1880

Prof. Dr. Virchow gave a presentation about the Eskimos today. The weather was nice. The garden was visited by approximately 16 000 persons. It was a cheap [reduced rate] Sunday, and the working people in Berlin usually wait for such days to visit the garden.

Fig. 38 Tobias, Paingu, Tigianniak, Ulrike, and Sara. (Illustration by Adolf Liebscher. Prague's Světozor Newspaper. 1880-11-26.)

---

[1] Newspaper articles and other types of records sometimes refer to this woman as Mrs. Jacobsen. Her identity has not yet been fully uncovered.

Stay in Prague and in Frankfurt

November 1880

Fell ill again in Berlin (with the old disease: cold fever ^{or intermittent fever}) and stayed in bed until our departure.

Monday • November 15, 1880

Departure from Berlin at 8 o'clock in the morning after a tender farewell from all acquaintances. The evening before, we had drunk the farewell toast with all acquaintances here at a restaurant.

Arrived in **Prague** in the evening. In Prague, our Eskimos were in Kaufmann's Menagerie, where two huts had been built, one for the Christian family and one for the heathens, just as in Berlin. Now it was better in so far as the huts had been built inside the menagerie ^{tents or booths}, so we had nothing to fear from weather. The working time for the Eskimos was from 11 to 12, 3 to 4, 6 to 8 o'clock in the evening. Visitors (numbers) in Prague were not bad, only that staying in a menagerie is anything but comfortable—after all, you are dealing with menagerists.

> *On margin:*
> Since Eskimos had never been shown in Prague before, the interest was quite strong. The press especially showed a lively interest in us. One day we conducted a mock seal hunt on a pond near the city with a

few seals that had been brought there. There were a lot of spectators present, to whom paddling a kayak and throwing the seal harpoon were demonstrated.

Fig. 39 Abraham and Tobias demonstrating a seal hunt.
(Illustration by Adolf Liebscher. Prague's Světozor Newspaper. 1880-11-26.)

Monday • November 29, 1880

Departure from Prague. Kaufmann's Menagerie also departed to travel to Munich, so we travelled together as far as Schwandorf, where we separated and continued our journey to **Frankfurt**, where we arrived on the 30th. On the 31st we sat up our exhibit and prepared everything.

Tuesday • November 30, 1880

Here, also, two huts were built for the Eskimos.

Fig. 40 Tigianniak, Nuggasak, and Paingu inside their hut.
(Illustration by Adolf Liebscher. Prague's Světozor Newspaper. 1880-11-26.)

Wednesday • November 31 [30], 1880

The whole time in Frankfurt, the weather was highly unfavourable, with unrelenting rain and fog—which, of course, affected visitor numbers very much.

Stay in Darmstadt

Sunday • December 12, 1880

Today, Noggasak (daughter of the old heathen Teggieniak from Nachvak) began feeling sick. Today is our last. In the evening, things were packed. The Eskimos and Mrs. Jacobs travelled to Darmstadt in advance with a moving van.

Monday • December 13, 1880

I and Mr. Schoepf dispatched the collection, etc., to Crefeld (because we are only staying in Darmstadt for three days, and from there, we go to Crefeld). At noon, left for Darmstadt where we found the sick Noggasak in a worse condition. But she refused to take any medicine.

Tuesday • December 14, 1880

At 8 o'clock in the morning, we awoke to the shout, "Noggasak is dead!" You may well imagine our shock. The physician diagnosed a rapid stomach ulcer as having caused the death. The poor parents did not stop crying from morning until evening. Of course, it also had a very depressing effect on the others and on us as well.

Thursday • December 16, 1880

Schoepf had meanwhile departed for Crefeld. Mr. Walter had been sent by Hagenbeck to attend the burial, which took place at 4 o'clock in the afternoon. It had been advertised among the public by the registrar's office, and on our arrival at the cemetery, we therefore found several thousands of curious people, who had come to see the burial. I had the parents and Abraham in a hackney carriage. I had the hackney coach drive up to the grave to avoid the throng. I led the parents to the grave. But since the mother broke out into loud crying, I let them board the hackney coach again and drove them home.

Fig. 41 Nuggasak.
(Illustration by Adolf Liebscher. Prague's *Světozor* Newspaper. 1880-11-26.)

Stay in Crefeld

Friday • December 17, 1880

Departure for Crefeld in the morning at 8 o'clock. The parents were quite composed and even became talkative while we were travelling the beautiful route from Mainz to Crefeld. I showed them the vineyards. The Rhine was very choppy because it ran very high, and at several places it had caused damage (by flooding). Arrived at **Crefeld** at 7 o'clock in the evening. We were welcomed by Mr. Schoepf and the director of the garden, Mr. Stickmann [Hermann Stechmann] who later became the director of the zoological garden in Breslau.

Friday • December 24, 1880

Christmas Eve. Had an order from Mr. Hagenbeck to buy varied Christmas presents for the Eskimos. The ballroom of the restaurant had been made available to us, and there we prepared a beautiful Christmas tree. After everything was ready, we let the Eskimos come in. They were quite heartily delighted, both at the tree as well as the gifts. (These consisted of underpants, vests, etc., and for Abraham a violin and for Tobias a guitar. In addition, each family received a large group picture that had been photographed in Prague). We ordered wine and were together until 11 o'clock at night, not knowing which cruel blows fate had in store for us. The weather had meanwhile improved a little, because in the previous week, it had been raining constantly.

Fig. 42 Concert hall and restaurant at the Bockum zoo (near Crefeld). Where Christmas 1880 was celebrated. (Polar Horizons' Collection)

Saturday • December 25, 1880

Beautiful weather, but in spite of it, no audience. The old Paingo has fallen ill overnight, quite suddenly, the same symptoms as with her daughter. We immediately called for a physician (Dr. Jacobi), who gave us the assurance that it was only rheumatism and that we need not worry.

Sunday • December 26, 1880

This morning, two physicians were here who examined the woman most carefully but could not arrive at another conclusion but that it was indeed rheumatism (the physicians come in the morning and afternoon). Today, little Sara also fell ill, complaining about being cold and vomiting. Were invited to Mr.

Möller [Carl Müller-Küchler] (the owner of the zoo). Spent a beautiful evening.

> *On margin:*
> How the doctor's diagnosis [was false] became apparent only later. In Darmstadt, we had believed that the young girl was suffering from a stomach ulcer and here now it was said that it was from rheumatism.

Monday • [December] 27, 1880

The woman is seriously ill, and may it not go with her as with her daughter. Sara is also ill. How will it all end? We were supposed to depart tonight but cannot travel under these circumstances.

Tonight at 7 o'clock, the old Paingo died. We all stood next to her. Ten minutes earlier the physician had examined her and gave us the assurance that it was not dangerous. We all then went down the steps to the coach, where we stood talking about the patient, when Mrs. Jacobs approached and told us to come immediately, because the woman was lying dying. She died one minute after we had returned. Peace be with her. She was a good old woman. The husband is very sad, of course, and expressed his wish to be able to accompany his wife and daughter soon.

> *On margin:*
> It is still a puzzle to me that none of the many physicians could recognize such a disease as dreadful as smallpox. Neither do I understand why none of us Europeans became infected, who after all, had been with the people constantly.

Fig. 43 Tigianniak, Paingu, and Nuggasak.
(Illustration by E. Krell. 1886.)

Tuesday • December 28, 1880

Today, the woman was dissected by three physicians, Dr. Jacobi, Dr. Zimmermann (junior doctor at the hospital), and an additional older sensible physician, whose name, unfortunately, I have forgotten—nothing was found, however, that allowed diagnosing a specific disease. She was buried in Bockum in the evening, attracting a large number of people. Her husband and Tobias attended. It is a dreadful time for us. I feel directly responsible for the people.

On margin:
There, the physicians removed the upper skullcap with the hair, to expose the brain. After the examination I took the skullcap with me and kept it.

Wednesday • December 29, 1880

The collection was packed, and, in the evening, everything was loaded (at the train station). Today, the physicians diagnosed that little Sara is suffering from **smallpox**, and a transfer to the hospital is absolutely necessary, which was achieved the same evening—I first had a hard fight with the parents, who did not want to part from their child. Had to seek help from Schoepf. Eventually, Abraham let himself be persuaded to hand over the child to the hospital; he followed her there himself, prayed with the child and parted in tears. Mrs. Jacobs stays with the child as a nurse. At 10 o'clock in the evening, everything was loaded.

Fig. 44 Alexianer Hospital, Crefeld, 1883.
(Courtesy of Alexianer Hospital, Krefeld)

On margin:
So now we know which disease we have caught, and what has caused the death of the other two. But where may the people have contracted it? We had not heard about smallpox anywhere.

Stay and Death in Paris

Thursday • December 30, 1880

Were at the station at 8 o'clock in the morning. Did not depart before 9 o'clock. I was almost surprised at the calm shown by the Eskimos. We travelled via Aachen, Erquelinnes, Namur and Saint-Quentin. At the French border, the coaches were filled to the brim with soldiers on leave. We sat so tightly packed like herrings in a barrel.

Fig. 45 Train station in Aachen.
(Polar Horizons' Collection)

Friday • December 31, 1880

Arrived finally at Paris at 5 o'clock in the morning. I must admit, it was the most tiring journey I ever did on a train. Our baggage and collection had to wait for another train at Aachen, and so we spent the whole day waiting in vain for our things. At 11 o'clock, Mr. Schoepf received a telegram from Hagenbeck which announced the death of little Sara. I must admit that it had a devastating effect on all of us. In the first moment I was totally at a loss because one thing had now become certain: smallpox was among the unfortunate Eskimos, and it became clear to me at last that the two others [Paingu and Nuggasak] had also died of smallpox—only that they did not break out in a rash—the more dangerous. The final hour of the old year was also to end in bad news. It was a sad year for me. May the new one be better, but the prospects are truly not very promising. The first thing we will do tomorrow is to have the people be vaccinated, because none of them were vaccinated in their old homeland, because there are no physicians there. Thus ended the old year.

> *On margin:*
> *Upon arrival in Hamburg, none of us had thought of having the people vaccinated. In 1877, I had the Greenlanders vaccinated in Greenland, but this time, it was forgotten. It probably had to do with my being sickly all summer, as reported before, and that upon our arrival in Hamburg, I had to go to the hospital myself.*

January 1881

Gave performances [at the Jardin d'Acclimatation in Bois-de-Boulogne] between January 1st and 6th—and everything went well during that time—and we began to believe that our previous bad luck was over.

Friday • January 7, 1881

Today, our little Marie fell ill and, indeed, with smallpox. Had the physician here three times. They were all vaccinated again with a fresh vaccine, because the first vaccination (on January 1st) had produced no results with any of them. Beautiful prospects, that!

Saturday • January 8, 1881

Today, Tobias and Teggieniak fell ill, and most certainly of smallpox. Preparations were made to transfer them all to the hospital. I also feel unwell myself. It is probably an attack of fever, because I am freezing most terribly.

Sunday • January 9, 1881

Today, Abraham also became ill. All Eskimos were transferred to the hospital St. Louis—and I was also given a room in the same shack for the epidemically ill—and I was rather ill, even without this terrible upset—because according to my own perception, not one of us will ever leave this hospital. The physicians saw us at 10 o'clock and confirmed smallpox in all four of them, but with me until now cold fever. The wife of Abraham has been spared until now, but cannot be moved away from her child. They all seem to suffer terrible pains. There are also a lot of French here with smallpox. In the afternoon, we had a visit by Mr. Schoepf.

> *On margin:*
> *In spite of my miserable condition, I went to each of my poor [and s]ick people and tried to console them. But here the sickness was obvious. The face was very red, the eyelid swollen as were the lips. They all [suffered] great pain. In short, it was terrible.*

Fig. 46 Ulrike and Maria.
(Illustration by Adolf Liebscher. Prague's *Světozor* Newspaper. 1880-11-26.)

Monday • January 10, 1881

This morning at 11 o'clock, little Marie died. She was everybody's darling. It looks terrible here. We are surrounded by sick and dying people. A man of about 40 years died in the room next to mine. Because ^{all walls} here are made only of thin boards, you can hear every moan and every sound. Although I am sick myself, I am not too sick to support, as best I can, the poor Eskimos, who have to suffer intolerable pains. And I have to admire the nurses,[1] as well as the nurses' aides, who spare no pain to help those afflicted. But with the Eskimos, it is more difficult, since they do not understand a word of French. Poor Teggieniak is asking for a rope to strangle himself because he is suffering terrible agonies. In this sickness death is hard indeed.

Fig. 47 Tigianniak.
(Illustration by Adolf Liebscher. Prague's Světozor Newspaper. 1880-11-26.)

Tuesday • January 11, 1881

Today, the old Teggieniak was relieved of his sufferings. The bodies are immediately removed to the morgue by the gravediggers and are buried the next morning. Most of the sick are lying in one hall, and the beds are only a few feet apart. Of course, the sexes are segregated. The women have a different hall. Tobias lay next to Tegieniak, and right after he [Terrianiak] died, he [Tobias] got up and covered the corpse ^{with a bed sheet}, despite being so sick himself that he could die at any moment.

> *On margin:*
> *I too stood by, but without being able to render any help, apart from perhaps giving the dying a last glass of water. Death is terrible, especially if people die in such huge numbers as here all around me.*

May be inserted on page 148 of my diary of the year 1881.

Yet another experience from the St. Louis hospital has stayed in my mind.

Fig. 48 Hopital St-Louis, Paris. Bichat Street entrance.
(Photo: France Rivet, 2013)

The cold fever (intermittent fever), of which I had suffered almost the whole summer, had come back to me in Paris. This sickness finally manifests itself in that I would usually have attacks of extreme cold in the evening, so that my body would shake from the shivers, and I would have to lie down in bed. Around midnight the cold would suddenly turn into a fever, and I would begin to sweat to such a degree that my shirt would be drenched in sweat. The matron, who from the first day had very warmly attended me, had [noticed] this and between 2 and 3 o'clock at night, when my sweating had abated, she herself or a nurse brought me a fresh shirt which had been heated in an oven, to change.

The matron had a kind of office where she wrote the prescriptions and where she stayed when she was not with a patient. She allowed me to stay there during the day, because, as I mentioned, the seriously ill who would have to die soon, were mostly taken to the room that had been assigned to me as a bedroom. Through our daily contact, we became rather well acquainted and sister Cécile even strove to convert me to Catholicism. One day she said to me that it was really a shame that an otherwise sensible human being was not a Catholic. I replied in jest that it would be much more sensible if the two of us got married. She threatened me with her index finger but otherwise was not offended by my joke. One evening again I had an intense shaking fit and fell asleep when it was finally all over and after having sweated heavily. At night I was woken up softly by someone shaking my arm. When I opened my eyes, I was looking into such a sweet face and a pair of deeply blue eyes looking at me with a half-serious, half-amused look, which I never thought to have seen a more beautiful face. Like the other nurses, she was wearing a stiff white headdress, so that I could only see her face when she turned her face fully towards me. My face must probably have expressed [my] admiration a little too much, because she rather hastily helped me out of the sweaty shirt and into the dry warm one. Then, she removed herself slowly by walking backwards and turning her face towards me. The whole thing appeared to me like a vision.

When I asked the matron the next morning where the young girl had come from, and whether she would be back, she just laughed, and said something like "I quite believe that you would like to have your shirt changed every night by that young girl." Another young girl was lying in the adjacent hall. She seemed to be suffering intensely, obviously in a delirium, because she kept on calling for hours a man's name, which I have now forgotten. When I had finally fallen asleep and slept for about an hour, I was suddenly awakened by the splintering of the glass doors that led from my room into the garden and by the cold wind and snow that blew into my room. I was sitting in my bed, staring at the broken door with the snow blowing inside, when *immediately after a nurse came in running, and calling: "Where is she? Where is she?" Soon, a few more nurses joined her, the doors were pulled open, and several nurses rushed out into the terrible snowstorm, to [look for] the gravely ill girl, who in her feverish delirium had rushed through my room and the glass door, to disappear into the blizzard in the garden.*

A short while after, I heard a terrible scream from the garden, and I assume they had caught her in the garden, and now brought her back inside. But she did not return to this ward, and the matron Cécile would not tell me where she stayed and whether she too had died like most of the others.

I believe that never in my life have I experienced so much in a few days, and so much horror, as in this fortnight[2] in the St. Louis hospital in Paris in January 1881.

Thursday • January 13, 1881

This morning at 2 o'clock, Tobias died after having suffered terribly. He was brought into the room next to mine yesterday, but the poor guy came into my room again and again. He could no longer speak in the end, because his tongue was so swollen. His face was frightfully distorted, his shirt was bloody all over (they all spat blood in the most horrible way). Since he was much stronger than the others, he had to endure much more than the others.

> *On margin:*
> *It seemed as if Tobias was always seeking help from me, because when the death struggle came, he threw himself upon me, who was lying sick in bed myself, though not with smallpox. With the aid of the nurses we then managed to put the corpse back into the bed of his own.*

Right after he was gone, a seriously ill Frenchman was brought into the same room. That poor man also wrestled hard with death. He tore up his sheets and could hardly be restrained. His neck was closed up ^{was swollen shut so that he could not breathe}. They virtually suffocate. It is an uncomfortable feeling to be looking at death eye to eye, especially if death is as agonizing as with these unfortunate ones.

> *On margin:*
> *When the death struggle came for the Frenchman, he stretched so violently that the bedstead tore apart, and the corpse with the mattress came to lie on the floor.*

Ulricke has fallen ill but does not want to be separated from her husband. We partly had to force her to go to bed in a small room.

> *On margin:*
> *All this I was forced to see and hear. It was enough to make a healthy person sick. Only the nurses always remained their same selves.*

Unfortunately, there is a young girl in the adjacent room who is very sick and delirious. Today, she knocked out her windows. She is in a sheer frenzy.

> *On margin:*
> *I had fast fallen asleep when I was awakened by the violent shattering of glass. It was the young girl who in her feverish frenzy had jumped out of bed, crossed my room in which there was a glass door opening on the garden, and she walked through the door which splintered.*[3]

Tonight at 9 o'clock, our dear Abraham died. I can hardly say what I feel. He and Tobias have given me the errand to deliver their assets to their relatives in Labrador. ^{Hagenbeck has faithfully executed this testament and added miscellaneous.}

Fig. 49 Abraham.
(Illustration by Adolf Liebscher. Prague's Světozor Newspaper. 1880-11-26.)

Sunday • January 16, 1881

Ulricke died this morning at 2 o'clock—the last of the eight—horrible. Should I be indirectly responsible for their death? Did I just have to lead these poor honest people from their home to find their graves here on foreign soil? Oh, how everything became so totally different than I had thought. Everything went so well in the beginning. We had only now gotten to know each other and begun to hold each other dear.

I feel a little better and am planning to leave the hospital tomorrow. I think the best I can do is to travel to Aachen and try the baths there, because I also suffer from rheumatism. I will not be able to go to Hamburg before I am certain that I do not carry the smallpox disease with me.

On margin:
When I saw to Ulrike shortly after midnight, I noticed that she too would end her struggle soon. I tried to comfort her, but she waved me off with her hand, as if she did not want to see me at all. That was no surprise, because she knew that all the others had gone before her. I felt guilty to a certain degree for the death of these unfortunate people, even if unintentionally. Had I not come to Labrador, they would still be alive like all their relatives.

Monday • January 17, 1881

Left the hospital today and took lodgings with Mr. Schoepf and Mrs. Jacobs in a hotel nearby. Went to the [zoological] garden today and saw to our dogs. I still feel unwell.

Thursday • January 20, 1881

Departure from Paris. Mrs. Jacobs, the warden, travelled to Hamburg by the same train. Mr. Schoepf and our friend Martinet brought us to the train station. So soon, and under such circumstances, was I to leave Paris this time. Fate is tough, but I have to take ^{bear} it however it comes.

To be inserted on page 150 of my diary of 1881. See 'Stay at the St. Louis hospital, Paris'

When my Eskimos had all fallen ill of a sickness, and I had the premonition that none of them would escape alive, and because I knew Hagenbeck so well to know that from now on and for a long time to come, he would not undertake a 'Völkerschau' [ethnographic show] again. We had bought the ship mainly in order to engage peoples for such exhibits. What could we do with it now? This thought went through my head constantly and it was perhaps also, in part, the reason that I could not quite get well again.

Already, while in hospital, I had hit on the idea to offer the ship to the ethnographic museum in Berlin, and myself as a guide, to be sent on voyages to collect because the museum had already bought various things from my earlier voyages. However, the museum in Paris (Trocadero) had acquired various things, e.g. had bought up all things I had procured at graves and elsewhere in Labrador, including the skullcap of the woman Paingo, which the physicians in Crefeld had taken off to look for the cause of the sickness, and which I had kept in my suitcase among my clothes (wrapped in paper). However, when I was leaving the hospital, a professor from the museum came to view the grave finds from Labrador. I then offered the skullcap to him because I now wanted to get rid of it. The professor accepted it with great pleasure, stuffed it under his coat, and marched off with it. I have wondered later, why I was not infected by smallpox because I had kept this skullcap for weeks among my clothes. Now, when in Aachen, I had enough time to think all things over, I wrote a letter to Professor Bastian, the director of the ethnographic museum in Berlin, and suggested to him the following. In Hamburg I wanted to equip the ship for several years, [i.e.] cover the bottom with copperplates, to make it suitable for voyages in the tropics. Additionally, I wanted to hire a helmsman and five sailors and sail to South America first. I myself wanted to make a detour down Patagonia from the straits of Magellan (Punto Arenas) and collect there. In the meantime, the helmsman and the remaining crew should collect at the /Pescares/ Fuegians,[4] on the islands and in Schmitz Sound [Smyth Channel]. Upon my return, we wanted to try to penetrate through Schmitz Sound and gather a collection of the Araucanians at the southern tip of Chile (Valdivia). From there, I also wanted to assemble a collection from the Easter Islands (that did not belong to Chile then). From there I wanted to travel north through eastern Polynesia, visit the various groups all the way up to Hawaii (which then had not been conquered by the USA either). From there, I wanted to take advantage of spring to collect in British Columbia, especially Vancouver Island and the Charlotte's [Queen Charlotte Islands]. The following summer, I wanted to visit Alaska, depending on how far I could reach during the summer. The following winter was reserved for Western Polynesia or eastern Melanesia, so that in the summer of the fourth year, I would touch the Kurelyan [Kuril Islands] Islands,[5] Kamchatka, and on the way south Sakhalin, to continue the collection later in Micronesia during the winter. I had calculated the voyage for six years, and the museum was to pay back the ship little by little and all expenses. I thought I would manage with 10 000 to 12 000 marks per year for provisions, salaries and insurance. Mr. Bastian liked this plan exceedingly well, especially because he himself had been to all these various countries. He also knew that, if it were at all possible to accomplish such a plan, I would do everything to accomplish it.

He immediately contacted the greatest bankers in Berlin to raise such a large sum. His thoughts were the following. As soon as a collection had arrived from us, a committee of six gentlemen would estimate its value, and the gentleman bankers would get back a part of their money, plus 5% interest. The following gentlemen agreed to the plan to lend the museum money: I) Isidor Richter;. II) Valentin Weisbach; III) G. von Bleichröder, Berlin; IV) August v[on] LeCoq Baptist Dotto; V). E.C. Francke; VI) Ludw[ig] M. Goldberger; VII) Emil Hecker; VIII) Wilh. Maurer, all of them in Berlin, and also Carl Reiss in Mannheim.

I occasionally received a letter from Prof. Bastian, in which he expressed his agreement with my plan, and also reported that he had begun the project. Of course, I also reported this to Hagenbeck and my brother upon my arrival to Hamburg, and both also agreed to my plans.

Fig. 50 Carl Hagenbeck around 1890.
(Wikimedia Commons. USA Library of Congress, Prints and Photographs.)

---

[1] The German word 'Schwester' may mean a nurse or a nun. In Norwegian, it would translate to "sykesøster" (sister for the sick). In France, until the end of the 19th century, the patients' care in hospitals was reserved to 'consecrated women' i.e. nuns.

[2] In reality, Jacobsen spent only eight days in the hospital (January 9 to 17).

[3] Jacobsen seems to be referring to the same event which he also described in his notes added after page 148 (see January 11).

[4] Indigenous inhabitants of Tierra del Fuego, at the southern tip of South America.

[5] Jacobsen must be referring to the Kuril Islands that stretch from Japan to Kamtchatka.

After the Inuit's Death

Friday • February 21, 1881

Arrived in Aachen and went to the *Hotel Carlsbad* [which was located] opposite the museum. Mrs. Jacobs continued her voyage to Hamburg. Staying in Aachen is expensive. But fortunately the weather has been good almost every day, so that I can go for walks. I have stopped taking quinine and instead I take arsenic,[1] of course, in small doses.

The doctor said that I will have to stay here for at least 6 weeks if [his] treatment is to be useful.

I pass the time by reading and once in a while I go to the theatre.

Saturday • March 5, 1881

I had a /illegible word/ time during the carnival season.

Departure from Aachen. Arrived at 10 o'clock in the evening at Düsseldorf. Continued the voyage at 12 o'clock.

Sunday • March 6, 1881

Arrived at Hamburg at 8 o'clock in the morning. I took my things to Mr. Hagenbeck and was received quite cordially, as always. Mr.

Hagenbeck is thinking of making a trip to London, and he invited me to accompany him.

Monday • March 7, 1881

Departure from Hamburg to London on the steamship *Vega*,[2] Captain [blank space]. Hagenbeck received a telegram from Captain Schw[e]ers that the steamship which was expected to arrive from South America had passed Cuxhaven with a large number of animals which were expected to arrive in Hamburg then via Rotterdam to London.

Mr. Hagenbeck let his younger [half-]brother ^{John Hagenbeck} travel with him; he was to make his first voyage. There were not many passengers on board [including] a Swedish captain with his sister on their way to China. ^{A very nice girl.}

> *On margin:*
> *I had taken quinine during all of the summer and did not feel any improvement, but I had a terrible buzzing in my ear [tinnitus],[3] and once in a while I shivered with cold and then I felt hot again.*

Tuesday • March 8, 1881

We had a storm with a headwind. The young Hagenbeck [John] was very seasick, so much so, that I had never seen anything like it. During the time at sea [I] had a pleasant /illegible word/ with the Swedish captain and his sister. But she too became seasick.

Wednesday • March 9, 1881

Stormy and unpleasant weather. The young Hagenbeck [John] is half dead due to seasickness. Saw land in the evening. It then quickly became /illegible word./

Thursday • March 10, 1881

During the morning arrived in London. Mr. Hagenbeck senior had arrived the same morning, and he received us as we landed near the Tower. Visited /illegible word/ and the animal house for a long time and the Zoological Garden. The animals whose arrival we awaited, had not yet got here from East India.

Fig. 51 The Tower of London from the Thames, 1886.
(Internet Archive/Arkivkopia/Tekniska museet. Unknown photographer.)

Friday • March 11, 1881

Beautiful weather. During the evening the steamship for which we waited, passed by Gravesend.[4] We had sent a representative on board in order to help look after the animals.

Saturday • March 12, 1881

In the morning, the ship arrived at the Victoria Dock. I went on board with some other people to get the animals, but I was able to leave the dock only during the evening, and because the ebb tide would not allow it any earlier, [and] we were able to get on the ship only at noon on Sunday after long negotiations.

Sunday • March 13, 1881

At noon, a policeman came on board in order to look at the animals. There were various leopards, black panthers, tigers, about 100 snakes which were between about 8 and 20 feet long, all sorts of birds and mammals such as gnus, antelopes, kangaroos, various kinds of pigs, 4 /illegible/ cows, orangutans, etc.

On margin:
Orang is the Malaysian word for 'human'; Altang means forest.

Fig. 52 Shipping Wild Animals in the London Docks.
(Author unknown. *The Illustrated London News.* May 21, 1864.)

At 2 o'clock in the afternoon, we finally were finished with this, and I visited my brother's brother-in-law /illegible word/ in the /illegible word/ telegraph offices of Reuters[5] employed Mr. /Rocks?/, he lives in Tottingham.[6] Had a pleasant evening.

Monday • March 14, 1881

Made everything ready for the sea voyage, for we wanted to leave already on Tuesday. (Hagenbeck and his brother [John] had already gone on their voyage on Saturday evening, travelling by land.)

Tuesday • March 15, 1881

Left London at 10 o'clock. The weather was nice and there were not many passengers on board; a family from the Cape (Cape of Good Hope).[7]

Wednesday • March 16, 1881

Beautiful weather. Had a pleasant day, as there was a very amiable woman on board. She is from [the] Hamburg [suburb of] Eimsbüttel.

Thursday • March 17, 1881

Arrived in Hamburg and had a lot of work with getting the animals ashore and to house them at Hagenbeck's. 12 of the mammals died on the way, but they had come on board in a very bad shape.

April 1881

We were in Hamburg from the 17th of March until the 1st of May, busy with all sorts of small jobs. In the meantime [I] was a couple of times /sick?/.

No voyages were made with the vessel [*Eisbär*] which is in the Dreyer Shipyard at Reiherstieg. It had been intended that the ship should go to South America and to the West Indies, but that [plan] was given up.

Fig. 53 Reiherstieg shipyard, Hamburg, 1840.
(Adolph Friedrich Vollmer, Wikimedia Commons/Public Domain.)

Sunday • May 1, 1881

Left during the evening with a load of animals for Breslau[8] via Berlin.

Two gnus and some smaller animals were destined for the Zoological Garden. During this voyage we passed through Berlin.

Monday • May 2, 1881

There was no opportunity to go on from Berlin that evening. So I went, of course, to the Zoological Garden knowing /illegible words/ that I would meet the Inspector [at the] Restaurant Schneider. I went with Mr. Pechler to the Elephant Building to see 2 young elephants from East India, which had been a present to the Berlin Zoological Garden from the Prince of Wales.[9] These animals were now being trained every day. I arrived there just as the animals were being led back into their Elephant Building. The two keepers were busy with the animals when I heard a scream. When I went closer to investigate, it became apparent that the larger of the two elephants had stuck a tusk through the right side of the chest of one of the keepers. The keeper still had the strength to get outside [the building], but then he fainted and fell to the ground. I bandaged him as well as I could, and he was then sent to a hospital. (Since then [his wound] has healed completely and was released again [from the hospital].) At 7 o'clock in the evening, I continued my voyage.

> *On margin:*
> The accident happened when the keeper tried to fasten a retaining chain around a foot of one of the elephants. I stood very close to the supervisor of the keepers (Pechler) and we did not notice that the elephant was angry. After we had removed the badly wounded man from the enclosure, I took off his linen shirt, tore it [into strips] and used [it] as bandage material.

Tuesday • May 3, 1881

Arrived during the morning at Breslau. We took the animals in good condition to the [zoological] garden. I helped with the unloading of the animals. Because the weather was bad therefore I took my leave and went back to Berlin.

Wednesday • May 4, 1881

Arrived in Berlin and visited Professor Bastian. I showed him a plan which I had thought of a long time ago, namely to either buy the ship [Eisbär] or to use it for a voyage for the Museum [of Ethnology in Berlin] in order to collect ethnological objects for the museum. He was very friendly and promised me to think about it. Professor Bastian has known me for years, as I had collected various things for the museum. I had been introduced to Professor Bastian by Privy Councillor [Professor Rudolf] Virchow. During the evening I travelled back to Hamburg.

I stayed in Hamburg from the 4th to the 8th of May.

> *On margin:*
> I had actually written up that plan already in Aachen, and then had sent it to Professor Bastian, but after that I had no communication from him. So, I visited him in Berlin.

Saturday • May 7, 1881

I got a letter from a Mr. Le Cock [August Albert von LeCoq]. He passed through Hamburg during a trip to Copenhagen, and I went to see him at the hotel where he stayed. There we had a conversation about [the possibility of] making a voyage for the Museum [of Ethnology in Berlin]. He told me that preparations were being made to get enough money to [lease] the ship [Eisbär] for 2 to 3 years, and to send it into the Pacific Ocean. Hagenbeck left 2 days ago for a trip to London. I will follow him tonight.

> *On margin:*
> *As can be seen from the list which was added elsewhere, Mr. Le Coq knew one of the members of the Committee which was supposed to supply the needed aid.*

Sunday • May 8, 1881

Left this morning at 3 o'clock on a steamship to London. In addition to many other passengers, there were 8 who had the intention to were emigrating to America. There was a lively crowd on board. Wind and sea were quiet.

Monday • May 9, 1881

Stormy weather with big waves. Almost everybody is seasick, especially some young girls on their way to London to seek jobs there as household help.

Tuesday • May 10, 1881

Stormy. Arrived during the morning in London. I followed William Jamerack[10] [Jamrach] to his home, and found the Hagenbecks there. The ship for which we waited, had not yet arrived. Was in the Zoological Garden with Mr. Hagenbeck.

Wednesday • May 11, 1881

This evening the ship arrived. Mr. Hagenbeck's traveller, Mr. Palfie [Pálfy?—a Hungarian name] [who is] a physician, brought

67 Hamadryas baboons or whatever they are called. He had caught them all himself in Abyssinia [Ethiopia]. He had originally 120 [of them], but the others all died because they had had a terrible /illegible word/. Mr. Hagenbeck bought very many animals here. I will take all of them with me ^{to Hamburg}, and Mr. Palfy will also come along.

Thursday • May 12, 1881

Brought all of the animals and also Mr. Palfy on board of the [name of ship is illegible] of Hamburg. All of the animals and reptiles which Mr. Hagenbeck had bought came from Mr. [Charles] Jamerack[11] and William Jamerack ^(two different companies at that time).

Friday • May 13, 1881

Left London to travel to Hamburg. Nice weather. We had a very pleasant voyage. There were various passengers on board.

Saturday • May 14, 1881

We arrived during the evening at Heligoland. But due to the wind and fog we could not land and anchored in the Elbe River.

Sunday • May 15, 1881

During the morning we arrived in Hamburg and were received by Mr. Hagenbeck. We were busy all day getting the animals onshore, and to get the animals accommodated. Mr. Kaufmann, the owner of the [Kaufmann] Menagerie was there, and bought various animals. ^{All of the rest of the month of May} I spent with Palfy, who made various purchases in Hamburg.

Tuesday • June 10, 1881

Mr. Palfy left today ^{for Africa}. I brought him to the place where the steamer /illegible text/ who went to China. There were many passengers on board. In the evening, after I had said goodbye to Mr. Palfy, I travelled back to Hamburg.

I made a short trip to Bremen because of the belongings of the ^{dead} Eskimos, and saw Mr. Missionary Elsner.[12] He suggested that those outstanding sums of money and wages ^{which had not been paid to the dead people by Mr. Hagenbeck}, be sent to Pastor Ludwig in Altona [a suburb of Hamburg]. The money was sent to Mr. Ludwig in Altona, who took care of this matter. Later on I heard that the ship which was meant to go to Labrador did leave during the middle of June.

> *On margin:*
> *The accumulated salaries of the Eskimos, as well as the clothes and other objects they had purchased were sent to the relatives of the deceased Eskimos, after everything had been disinfected. For Eskimos, it was already a considerable sum, and the relatives will have been quite delighted. It was told later on by the Moravian missionaries to Hagenbeck that the relatives were quite glad.*

Tuesday • June 21, 1881

I then travelled to Berlin in order to see what was happening about the business with the Museum [of Ethnology], because I could see that there was not much more to do for me at Hagenbeck's.

It seems to me that the death of the Eskimos has ruined ^{for a long time} [the business of] exhibiting exotic people.

Wednesday • June 22, 1881

Arrived during the morning ᶦⁿ Berlin. I had a meeting with Professor Bastian. The affair did not seem to have progressed very much in spite of the efforts which Mr. Bastian had made. Mr. Von Le Cock [LeCoq] has gone on a voyage to America, and there is a lack of money. And such an enterprise demands lots of money, ᶠᵒʳ even at the start of it I have to have several thousands [of gold marks].

Saturday • June 25, 1881

We were in Berlin until Saturday. We spent the whole day in the Museum [of Ethnology]. Mr. Bastian was very busy. But the prospects for equipping a ship have shrunk more and more. However, there is a chance that I will be sent to America, and especially to British Columbia. I travelled back to Hamburg alone.

Last week, Mr. Schoepf ʷʰᵒ ʰᵃᵈ ᵇᵉᵉⁿ ˢᵉⁿᵗ ᵗᵒ ᴬᵐᵉʳᶦᶜᵃ ᶠᵒʳ ᴴᵃᵍᵉⁿᵇᵉᶜᵏ, has now returned. He had travelled to the larger cities for Mr. Hagenbeck. During the time that I was there, his father [Albin Schoepf] died ᶦⁿ Dresden (he was the Director of the Zoological Garden and also a friend). He [Adolf Schoepf] has now been selected as Director of the Zoological Garden in Dresden.

July 1881

I helped my brother [Jacob Martin] in his store near the harbour until Sunday 24th then [went] to Hagenbeck's. Had little to do. I had received letters from Berlin in which Professor Bastian let me know that a committee had been formed with the /illegible word/ of the ethnological department to look over my collection and that I had been selected as a travelling representative.

Sunday • July 24, 1881

Received a letter from Berlin requesting me to go there. I left the same evening for Hamburg with more ^{confidence} courage.

In truth, it was no longer as pleasant at Hagenbeck's as it had been during the ^{earlier} years when I was there. It is probably all the guilt and that there is nothing more for me to do there. Hagenbeck, himself, has always remained the same as he had always been, but it is different with the family. They let me feel that I had spoiled it with them.

> On margin:
> Because the affair with the Eskimos ended so sadly, and we cannot do anything worthwhile with the ship [Eisbär], the Hagenbeck family no longer thought well of me.

SMALLPOX VACCINATION IN THE FREE CITY OF HAMBURG AND IN THE GERMAN EMPIRE IN THE YEAR 1880

By Dieter Riedel, M.Sc, Ph.D.

During the late 1870s and early 1880s, the medical and legal institutions in the Free City of Hamburg in charge of fighting infectious diseases seem to have mainly tried to cope with epidemics of cholera. In 1880, some medical authorities still thought that cholera and other infectious diseases were caused or that their virulence was determined more by environmental factors (such as 'miasmatic influences' or by the properties of soils) than by microbes. During the following 10 years, scientific and medical studies provided increasing proof that bacteria, viruses, and other microbes were the causes of common infectious diseases. In Germany, this progress in knowledge was hindered by the enmity between France and Germany and by a related refusal of some medical authorities to accept 'foreign' scientific and medical evidence of bacteria causing infectious diseases produced through the studies of Dr. Louis Pasteur, Dr. Robert Koch and other investigators. Koch and Pasteur tried independently to prove the validity of the 'germ theory' (Wikipedia 2018a), while other equally eminent physicians such as Drs. Emanuel Edward Klein and Max Joseph von Pettenkofer refused to believe in some aspects of that theory as late as 1892 (Atalic 2016; Evans 1973; Ogawa 2000).

In the early 1900s, the role of an apparently healthy cook who spread typhoid infections in the USA became widely publicized [see e.g., (Wikipedia 2018b; Leavitt 1996)]. That and other evidence revealed that some people may become 'immune' to disease-causing microbes and may not show any signs of illness. Later it became generally accepted that the severity of microbial infections can depend on the interaction of various nutritional, physiologic, immunologic, environmental and other factors which can help or hinder the multiplication of disease-causing organisms (Chang, Casio and Glass 2009). This observation applies also to people infected with smallpox virus [see e.g., (Behbehani 1983:485)].

The discussion below examines some of the legal, medical, and moral questions raised in connection with the preventable deaths of the group of Inuit from Labrador, who died of smallpox infections after they had been brought to the port city of Hamburg in Germany in 1880. They had been persuaded by the Norwegian Johan Adrian Jacobsen to sail with him to Hamburg to participate there and in other major European cities in 'ethnographic exhibitions.'

In considering these circumstances, one needs to be aware that the word 'smallpox' was used to name a disease which evidently was generally thought to be a lesser threat to people's health than the "great pox" or syphilis [see e.g., (Sefton 2008)].

At that time, effective smallpox vaccines were available in Hamburg, and an Imperial German Vaccination Law published in 1875 demanded that children, military recruits, and some other German population groups be vaccinated against smallpox. But that Vaccination Law did not apply to all residents of Germany, nor to foreign visitors.

In assigning responsibility for the deaths of these Inuit, one cannot simply apply 21st Century moral and legal standards to people and events of more than 140 years ago, because our ancestors lived by moral and legal rules which in part were very different from those which regulate our lives now. And using 'after-the-fact' (*ex post facto*) rules [see e.g., (Wikipedia 2018c)] to criminal cases in order to punish a person for something which at the time was not illegal, is actually prohibited in many countries [see e.g., (The Free Dictionary 2018)].

Scholars who have studied various aspects of the long history of smallpox epidemics are aware that our knowledge of the causes of infectious diseases, as well as the moral and legal rules aimed at disease prevention, have changed in the course of time. Felix Brahm stated (in translation from German): *The history of smallpox is told as if it were possible to retroactively inject our present knowledge of viruses as causes [of smallpox] and of specific, unambiguous symptoms [associated with smallpox infections] into the past.* (Brahm 2005: 294–295).

The contemporary report of a French Commission of Inquiry into the deaths of the Labrador Inuit in Paris (Colin 1881) wrongly implied that the mere act of passing an Imperial Vaccination Law in Berlin in 1875 would automatically have caused the immediate effective implementation of that Law throughout Germany, including in the Free City of Hamburg. A very rapid implementation of laws throughout a nation might have been possible in a unitary and centrally administered state such as France. However, in 1880 the German Empire was a federal state of more than 30 formerly independent Kingdoms, Grand Principalities, Principalities, and Free Cities, each of which retained a large degree of independent internal administration. Any new Imperial Law therefore had to be separately implemented and financed in each German state or Free City.

A relevant comment regarding Article 18 of the Imperial Vaccination Law of 1874 is quoted on page 50 in Carl Jacobi's 1875 official publication of that Law (Jacobi 1875). That quote states (as translated from German):

Section 20 of the Government Bill states in relation to Article 18 of the Law: "The regulations of this Law will become effective on July 1st 1875. The individual Federal States will provide the regulations which are required for its implementation."

Proposals (Motives) of Deputies added the following [explanatory text] to it:
"The implementation of obligatory vaccinations to the extent named in the Law depends on many conditions which will require detailed regulations. To these conditions belong among others the legal competence of the authorities responsible for the surveillance of the vaccination systems, the kinds of such surveillance, the implementation of controls of the vaccination lists, the creation and administration of vaccination localities,

and the budgetary provisions for covering the costs which are connected with them."

"In this regard it is neither possible nor necessary to formulate uniform regulations. Therefore this version [of the Law] leaves their implementation to the individual Federal States."

In regard to the implementation of the Imperial Vaccination Law in the Free City of Hamburg, Felix Brahm noted (as translated from German): *"The administrative authorities of Hamburg remained obdurate......and [therefore] Hamburg was one of the last countries within the German Empire to introduce obligatory vaccinations..... in April of 1872, an official Vaccination Institute had been opened. But the public remained skeptical... [The officially appointed 'Vaccination Physician'] Leonhard Voigt could not prevent that the German Imperial Vaccination Law which had been introduced in 1875 - which for instance prescribed that all children should be vaccinated during the first year of life - was implemented only very slowly....[in part because] ... even an Anti-Vaccination Association had been founded."* (Brahm 2005)

It is therefore not surprising that Carl Hagenbeck, the businessman who in 1880 had caused the Inuit to be brought to Hamburg, and who had himself had a smallpox infection in his youth, had not thought it necessary to have the Inuit vaccinated against smallpox upon their arrival in Hamburg. Nor did he think that it was necessary to have his wife and children vaccinated against smallpox until after the Inuit in his care had died of that disease.

Carl Hagenbeck and Johan Adrian Jacobsen had been jointly responsible for caring for the Inuit. Certain passages in copies of handwritten private papers of both men leave no doubt that like many of their contemporaries, they greatly underestimated the dangers of smallpox infections in people whose ancestors had never experienced this disease, and that they deeply regretted the preventable illnesses and deaths of the Inuit, and that they felt to some extent responsible for the sad fate of their charges. Passages in the German translation of the journal kept by the Inuk Abraham Ulrikab indicate that the Inuit could not have known that they had agreed to enter physical and social environments which were quite unimaginable for them, and which exposed them to deadly diseases.

The facts discussed above could lead to the conclusion that the deaths of these Inuit were largely caused by 'ignorant people exploiting their unsuspecting charges.'

---

[1] Up to the early 20th century, arsenic in small doses was used as a prescription medicine, as well as a 'tonic' by some people, although it was found to be a nerve and liver poison, and it can also cause lung, bladder and skin cancer. Source: Frith, John. Arsenic — the 'Poison of Kings' and the 'Saviour of Syphilis'. *Journal of Military and Veterans' Health*. Volume 21, N°. 4. Hobart (Tasmania, Australia). 2013

[2] Cathrine Baglo suggests that the *Veya* is most likely a Norwegian ship. It is the name of an island on the coast of Nordland. It could potentially be this ship: https://digitaltmuseum.no/021026957325/maleri.

[3] *Tinnitus* has many causes and can be an effect of overdoses of some medical drugs. See Wikipedia (https://en.wikipedia.org/wiki/Tinnitus)

[4] A town situated on the southern edge of the Thames Estuary.

[5] A telegram and news agency in London. In 1881, it was located at 24 Old Jewry. (http://www.thebaron.info/archives/history)

[6] A suburb of London.

[7] Now Capetown in South Africa.

[8] Now Wroclaw in Poland.

[9] In 1881, the Prince of Wales was Albert Edward who later became King Albert VII.

[10] William Jamrach, son of Charles Jamrach. Both were animal dealers in London.

[11] Mr Jamerack is believed to be animal dealer Charles Jamrach.

[12] Moravian missionary Augustus Ferdinand Elsner.

Excerpts From Johan Adrian Jacobsen's Other Publications

Excerpt from *Eventyrlige Farter, Fortalte for Ungdommen*

As noted in his journal entry dated September 22, 1880, in 1894, Jacobsen published a book in which he described the scene where Tigianniak used his powers to calm a storm. In fact, his book *Eventyrlige Farter, Fortalte for Ungdommen* dedicates a whole chapter to his travels with the 'Eskimos' from Labrador. Here is an English translation of that chapter. Translated from Norwegian by Hartmut Lutz.

The Labrador Eskimos

For weeks we had been lying still and had worked on our vessel in the drift ice outside the gulf of Cumberland. All the while the masses of ice piled up around us, so that the ship was lifted up or laid completely on her side. We expected every second to be forced to leave the skiff. Then one night a strong south-east storm arose, which drove the ice somewhat apart, but, on the other hand, it packed it together so tightly along the coast, that there was no chance of landing. It was only with the greatest possible care that we could get us /bautet/ [steered?] out of the ice again, and we decided to run into one of the fjords in northern Labrador.

One stormy evening we were in Nachvak fjord. None of the indigenous villages were marked on the map, so we did not know if the region was inhabited or not. It was dark, the fjord was full of violent waves, and black clouds chased each other in a mad race across the sky. Every once in a while, a giant rain shower would rush in. We constantly took soundings /and moved [?]/ with reefed sails. Finally, I hit upon the idea to fire a rifle shot. To our delight it was answered a short while later, and /from close by/, from the coast on the right. We fired again, and after /several/mutual? Gjentagne/ [(old spelling?) not in the dictionary] shots and answering shots from the land, we could finally drop anchor in a small bay, where the water was fairly calm.

Fig. 54 Head of Nachvak Lake.
(Painting by Arthur Philemon Coleman, ca 1915. Victoria University Library (Toronto))

Soon after, a boat filled with Eskimos came out to us. They immediately climbed on board without showing the least sign of fear. They were wild guys, at least judged by their looks. The men wore their hair long, hanging down to their eyebrows, and in the back, it flowed unkempt and wild over their shoulders. Short jackets of reindeer skin and sealskin trousers were their traditional costume. The women wear a jacket of sealskin which reaches down to their ankles in the back somewhat in shape like a beaver's tail. The hair is braided and rolled up around the ears;

braided into the hair they wear a long dangling tassel of pearls, which often hangs down over the shoulders in more than half an ell's length.[1] The forehead is tattooed with stripes, running parallel with the eyebrows. The rest of the traditional costume: leggins [or pants? 'benklaer' literally means leg clothes] and short boots.

Since the language of these Eskimos is rather similar to that of the Greenlanders, we could soon make us understood to each other, and so we learned that we were in the vicinity of a trading post belonging to the Hudson's Bay Company, and because of that, all the Eskimos were supplied with weapons.

We treated them to salted meat, hardtack, butter and tea. One after the other of the savages tasted the salted meat, but all of them together spat it out again immediately, exclaiming: "Tara juk!" (too much salt!). But the tea and the hardtack they seemed to enjoy excellently.

When they helped us the next morning to fill the ship's barrels with fresh water, they tied ten and ten[2] dogs before the sleighs and drove the barrels down to the lake on them, /because (? Skjönt)/ there was no snow. Later a few indigenous came along to pilot for us. It then happened so that just when we had reached a part of the coast, where there are many dangerous /baaer/ [?, not in the dictionary] and underwater reefs, it struck in with thick fog [?, not in the dictionary] and calm. We had high waves from the front, and the calm was not for the best. Some of the crew and the Eskimos were posted in the front of the ship, some up in the rigging to listen for /braendingerne/ [the surf?]. Because it had become night, and we saw no further than two ells. The ship was tossing in the hollow [?] sea. The ropes hung down limp and rattled against the yards and masts during the vessel's violent movements. The helpless passivity we were condemned to (endure) during this difficult calm was extremely painful. Each moment we could expect to hit the ground in this heavy sea and the crazy dark. Then suddenly a gust blew through the rigging. More followed after, the sails billowed; we heard the rigging creak and blocks rattle. From the distance came the sound of a mighty roar: the storm, which had only relaxed for a while, broke out with renewed violence.

At the same time, one of the Eskimos shouted forward from the aft: "The surf! The surf!" And close behind the back of the ship, we saw giant white crests of waves breaking over a long-drawn /flu/ [flood? stream? current]. We hastily dropped the anchor. The sails, of which the storm had gotten a hold, were taken down as fast as possible. When the vessel turned into the wind, we could have hit the coast with a stone. That is how close it was.

It was a night full of danger. The storm howled through the rigging. The ropes rattled and knocked, the blocks whistled, the ship creaked and surrendered, while the waves unremittingly washed over the fore deck. Right behind us thundered the surf, and we saw the white froth shine through the darkness. The sea boiled and roared all around us, waves slapped against the ship's sides, raised themselves high as if they wanted to devour us, and threw themselves loudly upon the deck. But nevertheless, the anchors held, and when the first grey of dawn appeared and the wind, at the same time, jumped a few degrees further east, we could leave the dangerous anchorage all in one piece.

One of our pilots, the others told us, was a shaman, that means a conjurer. He soon found an occasion to show us that. We had again come close to a coast that was full of riffs and surf, which we had the greatest difficulty to stay clear of. We pressed forward, with all sails close up to the wind, in order to get past that dangerous spot. I had just gone down into the cabin to check the maps when I heard a terrifying scream from the deck. I rushed up the stairs; I thought that nothing less than that a crew member had fallen down from the yard or something similar. But there were other things happening. In the stem of the ship stood the shaman—Terriaulk [Tigianniak], the old red fox, was his name—with wild gestures, with his face turned against the storm, so that his long hair whipped like a mane in the wind, with raging shrieks and incantations, which again and again drowned out the storm's thundering. At the same time, another of the Eskimo sat in the hatch and made the most surprising movements with the hands, but in the deepest silence.

Only after the shaman had carried on for a long time, so that he could hardly seem to have anymore voice in his life, did he stop with his screaming and his gestures. When I asked him what his surprising behaviour should mean, he answered ceremoniously that he had conjured the storm and that it would soon turn to our advantage.

Since the wind did really jump around after an hour, he grew extraordinarily in the eyes of the crew. Since then, they never called him anything else but 'Angakok,' the conjurer.

---

[1] An ale (in Danish) or Elle (in German) is the length between wrist and elbow, about a foot long, so half an ell would be about 6 inches (15 cm).

[2] Our assumption is that Jacobsen meant two sleighs were used to carry the barrels and ten dogs were tied to each sleigh.

Excerpt from *Ein Seemansleben*

In Jacobsen's archives at the *Museum am Rothenbaum – Kulturen und Künste der Welt*, we find a manuscript entitled *Ein Seemansleben* (A Sailor's Life). It was published in 1912 under the tilte *Aus den Jugendjahren meines Seemanslebens* (Jacobsen 1912).

We are providing Dieter Riedel's German-English translation of a short section of the chapter in which Johan Adrian Jacobsen talks about the first storm he had to face with his new schooner, the *Eisbär*.

The mysterious abandoned sailing ship

Experience had taught us that success in collecting ethnographic [or anthropologic] objects among exotic uncivilized people depends on having an easily handled ship of one's own, because one has to travel to remote regions away from heavy traffic, which are difficult to reach due to inadequate connections.

It often happens that a voyage planned one day has to be given up the next day, and then one has to wait, one does not know how long, in order to acquire some valuable object of whose existence one has become aware only at the last moment.

As on our first voyage, we intended to sail to the polar regions of North America, I went to Norway, where the Arctic seas are so to speak in front of the door, and where the best vessels in the world are being built for use in that region. Here I bought a schooner called 'Polar Bear,' which I let be equipped with a second layer of planks over its hull (a so-called ice skin) in order to make it more resistant to the sharp edges of drift ice.

That task was finished in mid-February.

We left with the help of favourable winds, but we had hardly reached the North Sea, when a strong southwesterly wind began to blow which soon veered towards the west, and then developed into a real storm. It became so violent that our schooner made the oddest movements. It stood almost vertically upon its stern, then dropped down to bury its bow among the waves, and constantly began to roll from side to side. But [our vessel] proved to be a real polar bear, which successfully fought the furious storm and waves. Apparently few other ships had been able to resist this hurricane, because we often encountered pieces of wrecks, an eloquent proof that human power had failed to resist the storm.

During the third day the storm began to weaken somewhat, and early in the morning we saw towards the west a sailing ship which made such odd movements that we changed course in order to have a closer look at it. As we came nearer, we could see that it was a schooner which had lost its masts during the storm, and which had been equipped with emergency masts by using reserve spars to which stay sails had been fastened.

The ship seemed to have been abandoned, and that explained the odd movements of the vessel, which had become a toy of the wind and waves.

[end of excerpt]

At the end of this short chapter, in which no date is mentioned, Jacobsen explained that the owner of the abandoned vessel had been a rich Englishman who also owned properties in Norway, and who, together with a crewman, had been swept overboard and drowned. The widow and the remaining crew members had been saved by a Danish schooner, and the abandoned vessel was finally found near Bergen by a ship's pilot.

JOHAN ADRIAN JACOBSEN'S CORRESPONDENCE

1880-07-07 — 1st Letter to the North Greenland Inspector

~~Hamburg~~ Jakobshavn, July 7, 1880

With this letter I would like to address the excellent Inspectorate for permission to purchase the following items:
- 6 adult dogs,
- 6 kayaks, like those I have seen in different museums in Europe,
- many kamiks and furs, partly for employees, partly for museums. We demand more than 6.

I would like to receive permission to take with me Okabak and his family to go to the West Coast (Cumberland), as well as another kayaker to help investigate the shores and examine whether the ice conditions allow it. This trip was undertaken to hunt whales but also to see what I could find as ethnographic objects among the natives. I await the response of the inspector. I'll stay here carefully until I receive it. Let me know as soon as possible!

Yours,
J. A. Jacobsen

1880-07-14 — NORTH GREENLAND INSPECTOR'S REPLY

Godhavn, July 14, 1880

Today, the Inspectorate received a letter from you, dated the 7th of July of this year at Jakobshavn, in which you asked permission to buy various things, and to also take along a couple of Greenlanders on your voyage. Although you stated that you were a whaler, you are obviously trying to find out what ethnographic objects might be obtainable here.

As you already know, from your earlier voyage, that these coastal regions may not be approached by ship nor be visited without a prior permission from the competent authorities in Denmark, it will probably not surprise you that in spite of the commendable favours which you did earlier for some Greenlanders whom you took with you to Europe because that was permitted by higher authorities, we are at present not able to grant your wishes, with some exceptions.

The Inspectorate absolutely cannot allow you to hire local Greenlanders to accompany you on your voyage. However, because of your earlier good behaviour, we will inform the Colonial Administrator at Jakobshavn that the Inspectorate can allow the purchase of merely 2 kayaks instead of 6, because as you must certainly recognize, buying up so many kayaks at once would deprive a number of Greenlanders of their usual income for a considerable time, until new kayaks could be obtained.

If you can deliver three copies of a written declaration to the Directorate responsible for the Royal Greenland Trading Company that on demand and when required, you will pay the difference between the prices fixed here for 6 Netsilik furs and 12 pairs of kamiks and for the furs at auctions in Copenhagen, then you may take them with you. You must also declare the number of furs and their condition.

Krarup Smith

1880-07-20 — 2nd Letter to the North Greenland Inspector

Jakobshavn, July 20, 1880

In today's mail I received the inspector's response regarding my request to buy kayaks and dogs and the permission to get people able to navigate with kayaks for a trip to Cumberland. I must note that it is very surprising that you do not allow Greenlanders to leave their country. It was only for a short trip of maybe a month and it was never my intention to go further. I thought the Greenlanders were able to act freely as they wish. It is well known that the people of Greenland have accompanied various expeditions and I was advised that the people here are Danes, therefore, they are 'private' individuals. Naturally, one should ask by what right you have the authority to prevent a Greenlander from leaving his country.

Each year in Europe, there are people who come from various countries. So far, we have never had the experience of a government refusing to allow them to travel unless they were obliged to do their military service, or if they were criminals. I have never had the experience of not being allowed to travel along the coast of Greenland. I know there are many whalers from England who, each year, visit these places and travel anywhere. Already, several of my companions have visited Godhavn on other vessels.

Regarding the decision of the inspector to refuse to let me buy kayaks, 6 dogs and 12 pairs of kamiks, I have taken note of your decision and I will obey your instructions. As this area is very little known in Europe, I will do my best to inform people about the conditions in Greenland.

J. A. Jacobsen

1880-11-09 — Letter from Carl Hagenbeck

Hamburg, 9 November 1880

Esteemed Mr. Jacobsen!

I just received the letter from Mr. Schoepf in which he wrote that, on Sunday, the seal should be hunted, skinned and eaten by the Eskimos. I urgently ask you to drop the first part of the program because I do not want the animal to be harpooned in the pond. The seal should simply be slaughtered. You will have received my letter of yesterday and I hope to receive right away a telegram to let me know when Philadelphia should come there. I'm glad to hear that the old Baengu [Paingu] is getting better.

With friendly greetings,
Carl Hagenbeck

1880-11-12 — Letter from Carl Hagenbeck

Hamburg, 12 November 1880

Esteemed Mr. Jacobsen!

I received your letter and learned from it, to my regret, that you have to stay in bed. I hope to see you again in good health and ask you to send me a postcard every day to let me know how you and the Eskimos are.

Friendly greetings,
Carl Hagenbeck

1880-11-13 — Letter from Edgar Bauer

General Administration of the Royal Museums

Berlin, 13 November 1880

Professor Bastian asked me to try to persuade you that the following objects of your Labrador-Greenland-Eskimo collections:
    1. Tambourine Greenland
    2. Music instruments
    3. Labrador snowshoes
    4. Labrador snow goggles

<u>objects from graves</u>
    5. Wooden figure (idol)
    6. Some stone tip [spear or arrow] and other objects
    7. Pearls

be added to our collections after they have fulfilled the use which you intended to make of them. We would also like to ask you about those [objects] which were made by Abraham.
[unsigned letter]

1880-12-26 — Letter from Carl Hagenbeck

Hamburg, 26 December 1880

Dear Jacobsen!

I just received the telegram from Schoepf that Mrs. Baingnu [Paingu] is ill and cannot be transported. Schoepf's letter of the 24th contains no comment at all about this and I ask you therefore to write to me immediately what is wrong with her and how long the physician thinks that all of you will have to stay there.

Greetings,
Carl Hagenbeck

P.S. I am writing to you because Mr. Schoepf probably will no longer be there when this arrives.

1881-01-10 — Letter from Henriette Kühne

St. Pauli, 10 January 1881

My dear good Johann,

I hope that by now you have received my letter which I wrote on 1 January and which I sent to Paris. I cannot understand why you would not have received my letters. I am proud to say that I have always answered your letters in the greatest hurry and on time. Please answer. I pray to God that you and the Eskimos may be spared the smallpox. I can assure you my dear good Johann that I'm extremely worried about you. It seems as if everything has conspired to prevent our expedition and I have lost nearly all my confidence especially if I think of the end of this unlucky voyage. Exactly at 12 o'clock on December 31 I thought of you and in my thoughts I sent you my best wishes. If only half of them were to be fulfilled my dear then you will do very well in this New Year. Tomorrow, I will send you the leather straps but I feel that my last letter to you has been lost. If you should receive my letter of today without any /illegible word/.

Now farewell but write to me **immediately.**

How are all of you doing? Our very best wishes, parents, sisters, brothers, and your
Henny

1881-01-13 — Letter from Henriette Kühne

[St. Pauli] 13 January 1881

My dear dear good Johann,

Once again I am trying to write to you, my dear. I am in despair because you do not seem to have received a single one of my letters. On Dec 22, Dec 31, and Jan 9, I wrote you letters and sent them to you from here. I certainly remember these dates and, in addition, there were 2 other letters which I wrote, in the meantime, but whose dates I cannot remember. I just do not understand how anybody can have the nerve to steal those letters destined for you, for that is what must have happened. My dear good boy you know me well enough that I do not have to forgive you if I /illegible word/ when I say that I wrote and mailed most of those letters myself. During these last years there has been almost too much misery and bad luck. I am mentally and physically deteriorating and do not think that living this way I can last much longer. I am very very worried about you, dear Johann. My throat hurts when my prayers remain unanswered. I do hope that this plague will finally be the last one and that you may be returning to our arms in good health. By now I have written so many letters, each of them emphasizing, dear good Johann, that we have had no news for the reason that you might think that you have had no news from us. Father just told me that you had written to him in order to find out what happened to us. He wrote immediately back to you and I really hope you will receive that letter. I am completely discouraged and I am almost out of my mind when I think of the situation in which you find yourself. I will try to write you this time at another address and I ask you, at the same time, to send me the address of the hospital so that we can address our letters in the future to that place. If I can find again Prof. Bogisic's address then I will also write to him and I will ask him to also inform you of it. Believe me, dear good Johann, we have not forgotten you and will always think of you. Why should we not be worried about you when your own dear life is in extreme danger? I am extremely upset that our letters to you were not passed on to you and I will ask the post office in Paris what happened to those letters. Reply to me immediately after I have mailed this letter. If you do not receive this letter, we will contact the German consul, or the German Embassy, in Paris. I will now close and do so with a heavy heart and an extreme worry. Please write immediately and I hope that the Dear God who has protected you so many times in danger may make it possible for you to escape again.

Best wishes,
Henny

1881-01-14 — List of Artifacts / Invoice for Prof. Bogišić

Eskimo objects which are to be obtained for Professor Boegisch [Valtazar Bogišić] (Paris, 71 rue des Saints-Pères)

1. One seal skin
2. One lamp
3. One woman's /illegible word/
4. One drum and the stick with which it is beaten (an instrument to accompany the song which accuses the enemies).
5. One pair women's boot without 'kolibak'[1]
6. One pair of boots for girls with 'kolibak'
7. A blue ribbon for the hair of ~~girls~~ women made of cotton
8. One pair of hair ribbons of seal leather for ~~girls~~ women
9. One /illegible word/ for ~~women~~ girls
10. A hair ribbon with seal leather for ~~women~~ girls
11. One stone weighing 2–3 pounds from the coast of Greenland
12. A /illegible word/ for a lance to hunt seals. Those with a sign on them are preferable.
13. A /illegible word/ badge of the ancient Angakok and if no genuine can be obtained then a facsimile.
14. A model of a fishing boat and other objects which once were deposited on the graves of the men.

15. A hatchet with handle (of wood, of bone or of reindeer antler) which was carried to Lubbock by the chief of a fishing expedition.

Invoice for Prof. Boegisch] [Valtazar Bogišić]

1 lamp	5 krowns 7—
2 women's ---- from Greenland and Labrador	" 4—
1 drum with drumsticks (gold)	" 8—
2 pairs of women's boots	16" 22.50
1 seal skin	1.80
1 stone	---
1 lamp with—letters	6
silk ribbons for the hair Greenland	1.20

	50.50

January 14, 1881
J. A. Jacobsen

---

[1] Jacobsen most likely meant 'qalipaaq.' In Greenlandic, it is a white piece of linen, generally embroidered, above the short women's boots.

1881-01-14 — Letter from Carl Friedrich Ludwig Kühne

Altona, 14 January 1881

Dear J. A. Jacobsen,

Concerning your esteemed letter which I received this morning, I hasten to write you this reply. Yesterday evening, the 13th of this month, the Jacobsen family was well and active, and we had fun including myself. Even the business aspects have not changed and that is all I have to say for the moment. For some time now I have been slow in answering your letters, but I will see to it that you receive as soon as possible an answer to your letter, and add what I forgot to include here. We found out through Henny that the awful illness is affecting the Eskimos. *Baengu* died of it. It is sad that these poor people died so far from their home and especially without being able to follow their own religious customs. At any rate, those among them that are still healthy [or "At least the other ones give the impression of still being healthy] which obscures their actual condition. At least they received some consolation and a bit of hope in addition to the care provided by the physicians which is also the only thing to preserve you. In addition to the awful illness, one now receives fear and shame. Both of those, one has to try to avoid. I recommend to you as well to reject any blame and responsibility for the illness which has killed them. It's bad that through this awful business you have been robbed of them and you have been so to speak incarcerated [kept indoors]. I hope it will not last much longer until this misery is at an end.

The business with the ship only causes us worry and anxiety. I feel that this matter will not be finished in the future without worry and problems. I wish that Martin <u>would get rid</u> of the whole business because it exceeds his ability and he may easily become hurt [it could harm him]. Perhaps this will last for a whole year.

But if you worry that you were responsible for taking these people away from their home and that they died because of it, this worry and this accusation are unfounded because you did not want to harm these people and you could do nothing to change their fate. The life of people, incuding that of heathens, is in the hands of our God. We cannot change his decisions. I will take your letters straight away to Martin as soon as I am done with my work.

With cordial greetings from all of us and my most sincere wish for a speedy recovery. I remaind your devoted,
C. L. Kühne [Henny's father, Jacob Martin Jacobsen's father-in-law]

1881-01-16 — Letter from Carl Hagenbeck

Hamburg, 16 January 1881

Dear Jacobsen,

I received your sad letter. You can well imagine my state of mind. I will follow your advice and will see to it that all of us get vaccinated in our house. I am less anxious because I already had a severe case of smallpox in my youth. But my wife is terribly worried and, therefore, I would like to ask you that both you and Schoepf should remain another 14 days in Paris. It is good that /illegible word/ go finish your affairs. You should just burn all the Eskimo objects and as far as the collection is concerned, I do not want it to come to Hamburg, because I no longer want to see any more Eskimo objects. I don't care how much anybody would pay, just get rid of them, of <u>everything</u> without exception.

Best regards,
Carl Hagenbeck

[On margin:] Show the letter to Adolf so I don't have to write another one.

1881-01-17 — Letter from J. M. Jacobsen and Henriette Kühne

Hamburg, January 17, 1881

Dear Brother Johan,

Your letter arrived. We are very sorry that you are in such a [bad] position. But dear brother, do not despair. Whatever is wrong now, may at some time still be good. I went to see Hagenbe[c]k and talked with him. I quietly told him what you had written to us. And he told me that he had been examined by a doctor. Keep to your position [or point of view] and defend yourself against those who stare [at you]. Had you not been really sick? I know that you wrote that you had symptoms of your sickness [*udslag*, i.e., a rash, or pustules] on your face, and that you were afraid of having that old disease [smallpox]. And Hagenbeck said that, of course, you were working out there [in a foreign land], which demanded a lot [of you], and that you would resent being treated badly. Better to put an end to it. It would be good if you were free of it.

And he said that I should write to you to tell you that! That was yesterday evening just after your letter arrived.

The last of the [illegible word] men has died, and now the woman is apparently dead as well. It is sad to think of that, especially for you, because you have had to hear and talk about it, when you are sick yourself. If I could come to visit you, I would really like to do that. But you know that it is difficult for me to find both the time and adequate means for that. I honestly would have taken anything that was worth buying [i.e. selling?]. I could have used my golden /illegible word/ as security [for a loan]. But Hagenbeck had just been examined by a doctor, who assured me that Hagenbeck would be able to vouch for you. You won't be a pauper. Hagenbeck told me that. He will write to you [to tell you] to sell all of the exhibition objects for what you can get for them, and to have everything burned that belonged to the Eskimos.

What now is to be done with the ship [Eisbär], I don't know. Recently, a broker was here and asked to see everything. And he thought that it would not be hard to sell it, except for the house. I can honestly say, dear Johan, that [selling the house for] 800 [marks] would be like giving it away to the man who bought it.

Goodbye for now, dear Johan, and get well again. Write soon.
Jacob.

[Added note along the left margin of the page:] In 14 days you will be here. That is what Hagenbeck said.

My dear good Johann

Yesterday we received your kind letter, and I am now relieved [to know] my dear good boy, that you have received my letters. And the telegram of the doctor in Paris, whom Hagenbeck had asked about your state of health, has taken a heavy weight off my heart. It certainly is very sad that the [illegible] affair has had such an end. But because almost all of them are now dead, then finally there is an end to it for the poor woman [Ulrike, the last survivor of the group of eight Inuit], if Our Lord takes her away as well. If you, my dear Johann, really [think?] that we have failed, then [take heart in remembering?] your courage and persistence with which you guided the care of those poor people, and that you were their last solace. Those good intentions may make some things better, though not <u>everything</u>.

Therefore do not worry and think about it unduly. Through our efforts and persistence we may, in time, be able to make good that which we have lost. What is most important, dear Johann, is that you will regain your health. I look forward to the day when we will have the pleasure of having you once again with us. Then I will come to get you at the railway station. Tomorrow I will notify the physician so that he may [get everything ready?].

Thank God that this last while we were able to complete some business. If God continues to send us frosty weather, then I believe that in spite of all those disasters, we will be able to manage it all. If some day your position with Hagenbeck should become doubtful, then you can come to us.

Now goodbye, see to it that you regain your health and hurry to come and visit us.

I am sending you many, many greetings with all of our love from your siblings, from our parents, from friends and acquaintances.

Henny

Notes about the January 17, 1881, letter from Jacob Martin Jacobsen and Henriette Kühne

By Dieter Riedel, M.Sc, Ph.D.

For several reasons, Jacob Martin's letter was perhaps the most difficult document to properly translate among all of those related to J. A. Jacobsen.

It seems to have been written in haste in the Danish-Norwegian typical of the late 1800s, in an irregular handwriting, but with some letters of the alphabet like those of the old German *Sütterlin* script, or so faint that they are hard to discern. Some parts of the letter seem disjointed. All this makes some of the text quite difficult to read and to correctly understand.

In contrast, the letter of Henriette which was written beside the second page of Jacob Martin's letter, is written in beautiful script in German, and expresses her ideas very clearly, which makes her letter very easy to understand and to translate.

Jacob Martin's letter may also have been written in anguish, because he postponed telling his younger brother some very bad news until the very end of his letter. In 1879–1880, the ship *Eisbär* had cost the family at least 15 000 gold marks. At that time, one Mark was worth 358 mg of pure gold (Wikipedia 2018d) (or in 2015 currency, about 101 US dollars). Therefore in today's currency, 15 000 gold marks would be worth about 1 500 000 US dollars.

Much of that money would probably have been borrowed. In addition, there would have been the cost of the lost load of guano due a leak after the ship was refitted in Norway, and the considerable expense of the ship sailing with a hired captain and crew from Hamburg to Labrador and back to fetch the Inuit. Even though Carl Hagenbeck might have paid part of that cost, the Jacobsen family now apparently needed to sell the *Eisbär* to pay off their debts. But a broker who had "asked to see everything" (on the ship, or all that which they owned?), had told Jacob Martin that "it would not be difficult (?)" [*swert*, maybe a form of the German word *schwer*] to sell the [illegible word] business, except for the [deck?] house, which apparently was appraised at only 800 marks. Jacob Martin thought that selling it at that price would amount to "giving it away" to the buyer.

Considering the great financial difficulties of the Jacobsen family caused by Johan's disastrous business venture with the ship, the most remarkable aspect of both Jacob Martin and Henny's letters is their consistently comforting and supporting tone, which suggests that they still loved and wanted to console Johan Adrian in spite of the great financial and emotional troubles which he had caused them. That also suggests that Johan Adrian Jacobsen must have been a good and lovable man.

1881-01-20 — Letters from Edgar Bauer and Adolf Bastian

/Berlin?/, 20 January 1881

My good Mr. Jacobsen,

Yesterday I went to Mr. Hagenbeck in the circus and he told me of the great misfortune. I cannot but tell you that I am very sorry about this and give you our heartfelt sympathy. How hard it must have been for you considering your friendly disposition and your sympathy to those good people quite apart from the business aspect. I'm glad that these terrible days have passed during which one person after another sank to the ground [died]. Absolutely awful! My good man! Because you are already /illegible word/, when I heard this, I could not help but to start to cry. Also, what happened could not have been foreseen. However, you ought to get over it and to resolve to move on.

I am adding a letter from Dr. Bastian who wants the objects from your collection. Idols, the wooden idols [included a hand-drawn sketch of an idol], Indian snowshoes from Labrador, /illegible word/ from Greenland, beads from Greenland, [...]

I assure you of my very great sympathy. Also, say hi to Mr. /illegible word/
Bauer

Berlin, 20 January 1881

Esteemed sir,

I just received the notice that all of the persons of the group of Eskimos exhibited by you originating in Labrador have unfortunately died. I therefore permit myself to enquire about the order from Mr. Bauer last November of several objects which had been exhibited with the group and which are part of the ethnological collection from that locality.

Please permit me to express again my vivid regrets about the misfortune that befell these persons.

I do not doubt that you will want to have these desired objects remain in our collection.

Respectfully yours,
A. Bastian

1881-01-23 — Letter from Adolf Schoepf

Paris, January 23, 1881

Dear Mister Jacobsen!

Today Saturday, I received your kind letter and I am delighted to hear that you've arrived in Aachen and also to see that you feel as good as circumstances allow. I did not have much luck so far with the sale of the objects. Tomorrow morning at 10 o'clock I expect Mr. [Armand] Landrin who announced his visit by letter and would like to see the objects.

Hopefully he will take many of them. Two gentlemen /came?/ yesterday for the kayaks, one of them wrote today about it but none are sold yet. Last night with Martinet I went to get your shawl and [I?] also set aside for you stone spikes [= arrow spikes made of stone?]. In the coming days, Carl will be going to Vienna. It seems that they are now serious about the people from Tierra del Fuego. We will supply some of them, that is to say, if they arrive home safely on March 10. Geoffroy [Saint-Hilaire, the director of the Jardin d'Acclimatation in Paris] takes them willingly. If you change hotel, I beg you to let me know.

Best regards,
Yours,

Ad. Schoepf

P.S. [written by someone different]

I am pleased to hear that you arrived <u>relatively</u> relaxed and rested in Aix[-la-Chapelle]. I hope you will not stay there for long, and that you will return soon completely cured in Hamburg or Paris. Cold and snowy weather here. It is sad that the Eskimos are not here.

Best regards,
Yours,
Martinet

1881-01-24 — Letter from Adolf Schoepf

Paris, 24 January 1881

Dear Mr. Jacobsen!

Enclosed are two letters which I opened yesterday because I thought that the people in Berlin would want to obtain more of the collection and, if you had mailed the letters to me later, then it might have already been too late. We now know that people in Germany have learned about the death of the Eskimos, as I could read in the [German] newspapers which have copied the French newspapers.

You are not writing anything about how you are doing with your cold fever; I really was afraid that you would be unable to get to Aachen. Was it really the old woman [Mrs. Jacobs] who became ill on the way? I hope that she will not bring the pox to Hamburg. Today, I unpacked everything and put it in order in the house in which the dogs are kept. I threw away the wooden boxes and I found [in them] many objects which had belonged to the dead people who, of course, will have to be burned. Among them, I found the beads and the /wooden figurine?/ which I retained for the Berliners [Adolf Bastian and Edgar Bauer]. The Berliners are enquiring about the models which you still have but which you did not record. If Landrin does not take them, they may have them in addition. Landrin unfortunately did not come today. None of the things have been sold yet except for the reindeer [caribou] skins [which were sold] for 40 francs to the people in the garden [Jardin d'acclimatation]. This evening I will go with Martinet to rue Blanche. It appears that there is another director there.

When I return to Germany via Aachen then I will visit you. Please write to me often. Have you gone to the Rehms Square yet?

Best regards. Yours,
Ad. Schoepf

1881-01-27 — Letter from Carl Hagenbeck

Hamburg, 27 January 1881

My dear Jacobsen,

I have received both of your letters and it is very reasonable of you that you stay in Aachen in order to /illegible word/. From all my heart I wish you will get better and I hope that the next letter will bring better news and that you will be completely healthy again. As far as the collection is concerned, I don't care about it at all. You and Schoepf can sell what you want. If you need more money just write to me and I will send you some. I hope with all my heart that you will get better.

Carl Hagenbeck

[On margin (written by someone else):] Many greetings from the family. I'm very busy...

1881-01-27 — Letter from Henriette Kühne and J. M. Jacobsen

St. Pauli, 27 January 1881

My dear Johann!

We just received your dear letter and I'm in a hurry to answer it immediately. Hagenbeck arrived here at the dock but he had to immediately depart again yesterday from Bremenhaven. He is supposed to be back Sunday evening. But as far as the money business is concerned, please <u>do not worry</u>, you will get it one way or another. Martin will go on Sunday, that is to say the day after tomorrow, to see you because before that he cannot be back from Bremenhaven in order to hand you your letter personally. If he would be unable to meet you then we will sell our watches. One way or another, we will see to it that you get it so don't worry about it.

Just don't worry, dear Johann. I hope that Hagenbeck will send us the money by telegraph. I hope Hagenbeck will give us the task of photographing the Patagonians when they come here, so that we will earn at least a bit of money, because the sale of the studio will take quite a bit of time. Pray for us dear Johann that we will have a thaw ["better future"] in order that we can get ships because otherwise our future looks dark. Once Hagenbeck will have sent you the money, then let us know immediately, so that we are at least rid of that worry. My dear good Johann, I send you my wishes for a speedy and complete recovery and hope to see you again very soon.

With my most cordial greetings and kisses. Your
Henny

Dear Brother
We're happy that you are better and not /illegible word/. I went to see Hagenbeck yesterday it was impossible to talk with him because Dr. /illegible word/ was to give him medicine. Hagenbeck was to go to Bremen. I was not able to talk to him about the ship. You will have been late with /illegible word/. Could not get any news out of Norway before we got together. Hagenbeck does not want to have anything to do with it. We have decided to send the ships to Iceland and from there to Hörten [Horten, harbour city near Oslo]. We'll have to hire a crew of at last two men from Tromsø. Having difficulty doing it.

[Jacob Martin's writing is very difficult to decipher in the remainder of the letter.]

Brother Jacob

1881-01-27 — Letter from Adolf Schoepf

Paris, 27 January 1881

Dear Jacobsen!

You will probably have received my letters and I received the one that you wrote. It really looks iffy about the money, dear Jacobsen, I still have 10 francs. I really don't know yet where I'm going to get the next load of money. Not a single object has been sold yet. I still have not met with Landrin either in the Trocadero, in his apartment, nor in the newspaper office.

This evening I will try once again at the office. I have handed in the bill for the object of the Laplanders. If I get that money, I can help you otherwise not. Mr. Hagenbeck probably loses money not only because of the thief Steiner, who is now in Geneva, but also because of Kreuzberg who either just went bankrupt, or put the menagerie under the name of his mother-in-law. That was the reason Mr. Hagenbeck was in /Vienna?/.

The few hundred francs which I still have here on our account, I will need here and for the trip when I travel with the objects to Germany. I can assure you that I will do my best to help you.

Today, the 4 English women asked about the Eskimos and they regretted that they are all dead. They also asked about you. The little Lucie will write you this Sunday and I told her that I will write to you.

Best regards,
Ad. Schoepf

1881-01-30 — Letter from Albertina Lutz

Munich, January 30, 1881

My dear Adrian,

I just received your dear letter for which I have waited such a long time. I thought that you might not think worth it anymore to think of me but all that is over now and I am again quite happy with you. I am very sorry that you, my love, are sick and I wish you with all my heart that you will soon be well again. You wrote in your letter to me whether I had forgotten you or whether I had ever loved you and that I have to confess openly my love that I will never forget you and I'll love you forever. I'm very sorry that the poor Eskimos all died but that can't be changed. I hope dear Adrian that you are in good health. I can say the same for me. However, the business is not as good as it should be. I think back to Prague when for the first time I felt what love is but that love was soon troubled by shadows and only the words in your letter could console me. Whoever will be in love will suffer but my love, I have to close now, I will have to write to you another time.

In the meantime, a thousand greetings and kisses from your loving Albertina. Please write to me very soon but also send the letter to Helena's address there where it certainly will get to me. The address is:

Helena /Josephsson/
18 Dampfschifpstrassen
Munich

Miss Albertina Lutz
Munich Bavaria

1881-02-05 — Letter from Edgar Bauer

General Administration of the Royal Museums

Berlin, February 5, 1881

Dear Mr. Jacobsen,

Just now your mail from Aachen arrived, at least I suppose it is from there, because we didn't expect anything else from Aachen, and the freight declaration seemed to have been written by you. (Sidebar: That is the state of affairs as we already have found out.)

At that time, Professor Bastian will probably have informed you of it as well and any further negotiations will be made by the buyer himself.

The Parisian objects have not yet arrived but I'm still hopeful that they will arrive and that they were not lost during the catastrophe [the death of the Labrador Inuit].

Please do not take this sad affair too much to heart. The thought which you recently mentioned is reasonable but, however, one could assert that even though you brought these people over here on speculation, they did not do too badly and, on the contrary, ^{they even became rich}. They came voluntarily and you were eager to see to their welfare and you did your best as long as they were in your care. One also has to consider that you were not the only speculant. You were also an <u>important servant</u> of the economy of which it is to be hoped <u>that you will be preserved and active for a long time yet</u>.

According to the medical examinations the state of your health does not seem to be worrisome.

Friendly greeting.
Your most devoted,
Bauer

P.S. I have opened the letter because I thought it might contain business information.

1881-02-07 — Letter from Carl Friedrich Ludwig Kühne

Altona, 7 February 1881

My dear Jacobsen,

Although I have heard from Martin and Henny that you have gone from Paris to Aachen, I was glad to hear that your health is beginning to improve. I received your letter dated the 5th of this month in which you expressed the hope that you would soon be healthy again. You have experienced an awful lot here and just to think of it that you had so many bad things happen, they suffice for a lifetime.

The business with the ship still causes worries and you seem to be in great danger. We were afraid that you might have lost your life. Basically, now you have no fund, no income, no prospect for the future in spite of past successes. We hope that this year will turn out better for you and bring more happiness.

/illegible word/ that would be the last ones, but what could you and Martin gain from it? Both of you /illegible word/ costs and loss of interest payments. The circumstances for you are most unfavourable. That enterprise only brought you unhappiness. One can expect further change for you and Martin. Both of you ought to get rid of the ship to gain something out of the danger and the risks that you took, but it's unlikely that you will profit from it because Hagenbeck has the greatest share in this ship and because he also has a right to most of the equipment and Martin has no way to pay. Hagenbeck will take the whole thing and then he alone is in charge and can do things the way he likes without having to ask others. Credits for 1 500 marks have been paid in cash and the rest Hagenbeck would pay in 3 months. That would help you but how <u>will Martin get himself out of this mess?</u> Martin cannot work because he has cancer. Do whatever you can. In addition, the interest for his loan is lost money just when Martin needs it so badly for his business. I see no other way out and I hope Hagenbeck, considering the circumstances, draws the right conclusions.

I and my family wish you all the best. Write me soon!

Your faithful friend,
C. Kühne

1881 - Letter from Henriette Kühne

[Undated except for '1881' handwritten in pencil in the top left corner]

My dear Johann!

This addition to my letter I am writing after receiving your letter and I am now somewhat comforted to know that you yourself, dear Johan, have not gone on the trip to the Arctic. Martin still has his illusions. Yesterday, I received the same kind of communication from Johann Hansen and sons in Tromsø. In that letter they talk about buying a sloop of [Fridtjof] Nansen's, the *Isbjornen* [Polar bear]. I hope that Martin won't again be duped. He talks about /illegible word/ who gave him a contract, but I have a holy respect for Martin's spirit to go into speculations. Hagenbeck has paid 1 500 marks for you. The other half he will pay only in 3 months. I do not believe, dear Johan, that we will be able to keep our part of the ship. As you know, we have obtained 3 500 marks from the Credit Union and we promised to pay the Horstens back the money we borrowed to buy the ship within one year. In the month of March, we must at least pay part of it back but I have no idea where we are going to get that money. My dear Johan, if Hagenbeck is going to pay you for the trip please ask him whether he is inclined to take over our share. Of course, he does not have to pay us the money in cash. If he refuses to do this, then we will have to see whether we can find somebody else. My dear Johan, when you return to our home then we will, of course, talk about it among us. You will certainly understand that we here do not consider as a blessing to keep the secret any longer. If we do not repay the 3 500 marks obtained from the Credit Union then my father, who was the guarantor for us, will have to pay, of course, and you can well imagine that I want to avoid this at any price. Just thinking of it makes me quite ill. Recently Hagenbeck is supposed to have made a great profit and it is my hope that, in the end, he will do what he promised. If the Eskimos had survived then we would have had the money for the voyage. As things stand now, it is very unlikely that we will earn anything. A thick letter addressed to you has arrived from Tromsø. Martin... I hope that by now you will finally have received the money (200 marks) which Hagenbeck has sent you. You cannot guess my dear Johan how awful I have felt recently among exotic people without the least bit of money. We now know what it feels like to be short of money.

Keep well, my dear Johann. Write me tomorrow. Best wishes.

Your
Henny

P.S. If you have time, and inclination, please write me a few words on paper. I would be <u>very happy</u>.

1881-02-15 — Postcard from Adolf Schoepf

Dear Friend,

Just arrived here. Today, I visited your brother and I delivered to him the glass syringes. The child is ill but not dangerously so and I hope that you are well. I have gone from Paris to Vienna, Pest [Budapest], Vienna, Hamburg to Bremenhaven and back to Hamburg.

I hope today to reach Hamburg. The objects are still all in Paris not yet sold.

Best wishes,
A. Schoepf

Mailed from Hamburg.

Addressed to:
Mister Joh. Jacobsen
Hotel Carlsbad
Aachen
Camphansbadstrasse 15

1881-02-17 — Letter from Carl Hagenbeck

Hamburg, 17 February 1881

Dear Jacobsen,

I read your letter to Schoepf and I cannot understand why you are so discouraged because you are usually so courageous. First of all, you must do me the favour and do not give up. Keep a level head and most importantly do not stop your treatment too early. Continue as long as the doctors think necessary. If you run out of money, just write to us how much you need and I will send it to you immediately. I hope to pass through Aachen in 14 days from now and might be able to see you then at the railway station while I'm passing through.

I very cordially wish you an improved state of health.
Carl Hagenbeck

1881-02-17 — Letter from Adolf Schoepf

Hamburg, 17 February 1881

Dear Jacobsen!

I have let Mr. Hagenbeck read your letter and enclosed in this letter you will find an answer to it. Take courage. I have to leave on a voyage today. Therefore I cannot write to you very much.

If you need money, just write to us and I assure you that everything is not as bad as you think.

Your Adolf Schoepf

1881-03-27 — Letter from Edgar Bauer

Düsseldorf, 27 March 1881

My dear Mr. Jacobsen!

I was very glad when I received your letter today in which you say that you are alive and well. I had very serious worries about you especially because my earlier letters to you had not been answered. In the mean time you will have received news from Mr. Hagenbeck that I have been given a position at the Royal /Academy?/. Here I have met several of your countrymen who talked about you in favourable terms. I have your dear letter and have written immediately to Professor Bastian. You do not have to worry about your grammar because you are a foreigner and to write in German is <u>very difficult</u> for any foreigner. I have asked Bastian to offer you <u>good</u> prices especially because you <u>support his ability to be active as an ethnologist</u> and you are able to provide a <u>very important</u> service for him. The second half of your letter with the greetings to /illegible word/ I will pass on your greetings to him. He will be glad to hear from you.

Finally, I hope that during your voyages you will occasionally visit me.

In the meantime, I send you my best wishes and hope that your expedition will be crowned with success and good luck.

Your devoted and /illegible word/
Bauer

1881-04-04 — Letter from Adolf Bastian

Berlin, 4 April 1881

Esteemed Sir,

The General Administration [of the Prussian Royal Museums] thanks you sincerely for handing over the objects of the Labrador Eskimos, which we received from Mr. Schoepf, and which came from Paris and Hamburg. The Commission of Experts estimated its value as 100 [gold] marks, which you will receive from the funds of the Royal Museums by a postal money order.

For the Director of Ethnographic Collections,
A. Bastian

Mr. Jacobsen, Esquire
At Hamburg

1881-04-05 — Letter from Adolf Bastian

Berlin, 5 April 1881

Honoured Sir:

The objects from Labrador which Schoepf sent have arrived in good condition and as Mr. Bauer lets me know from Düsseldorf that the commission of experts looked at the objects and approved the sum of 100 marks which has already been sent by the Royal Museum.

Please keep in mind the interest of our museum.

Your very devoted,
Bastian

1881-09-23 — Letter from Carl Hagenbeck

Hamburg, 23 September 1881

Dear Mr. Jacobsen,

I received your letter of 29 August mailed in San Francisco and I'm very glad that you are well. Here in our shop everything is the same. The only news I can send you is that Captain Schweers has arrived accompanied by 11 Patagonians who are now in Paris and have caused immense public attention. On a single Sunday, over 50 000 visitors came to see them. They are 4 men, 4 women and 3 little girls of 1, 2, and about 3 years of age. They do not wear any clothes but some animal skins instead. They eat meat and mussels that have been warmed up in a fire. They only drink pure water. I am sending you also an extra volume and an article about the people of Captain Schweers. In the way of ethnographic objects, he brought along only small objects /canoe?/ therefore it was good that I still have my beautiful collection. We will stay in Paris until 16 October and from there we will go to Berlin. The people shoot with bows and arrows and their lances and throw stones with a sling. But they are exceedingly lazy and their dearest occupation is to eat as much as they can.

Hoping that I will meet you in the best of health.

Yours,
Carl Hagenbeck

1881-12-02 — Letter from Carl Hagenbeck

Hamburg, 2 December 1881

My dear Jacobsen,

This morning I received your letter and most of all I am glad to know that your health has improved. You can't imagine how much your letters of 18 September and 3 November interested me. Your letter which arrived today I have already read 3 times and I intend to read it several times more because since this morning I cannot think of anything else but of the Indians whom you think you will be able to bring with you. I therefore beg you to come back to Europe once you think that you have done enough. Then you can be employed again by me because, thank God, since the Patagonians were here things have changed here. The business [profits] in Berlin and in Paris were really enormous and I have once again become encouraged. In Paris, the Patagonians were visited by more than half a million visitors. In Berlin, I had twice the success in 6 weeks as we had with the first Eskimos [the 1877 Greenlanders]. In addition, the animal business progresses very well and since you left, I travel almost all the time. Thank God the Patagonians are mostly in good condition but we lost the littlest child in Paris. If you were able to return already during the summer in June, July, or August then I would like you to bring along 8–10 Indians together with a small collection [of ethnographic objects]. Please let me know what you think of it. If so, I would be able to make available to you 1 500–2 000 $ for the voyage. I would also pay you your salary just as before, and in addition, a percentage of the overall income so that, at any rate, you will make a good profit. If possible, we would like men, women, and children. Please let me know what you think.

Best wishes also from my wife,
Carl Hagenbeck

The *Eisbär*

SHIP'S REGISTRATION DOCUMENTS

[The parts of the documents which were handwritten appear in italics below.]

Page 1 of 11

No. *1136*

Date of the record: *9 April 1880*

Date of the certificate: *9 April 1880*

Recognition Signa: *RFVM*

Declaration concerning the registration of a ship in the Ship Registry

Name of the ship: *Eisbär (operated earlier under the name 'Hevnegutten' [the boy from Hevne] under the Norwegian flag)*

Type and rigging of the ship: *Galeas*
(If a steamer, indicate [the mode of operation] whether by [shovel] wheel or propeller. Also, the total horsepower of the engines nominal: _____ actual: _____
The nominal (power) and, if known, also the actual.

Number of masts: 2

Principal Material: - Iron:
                      - Hardwood:
                      - Softwood: *Fir wood*

Bolts used   - of copper or metal:
                      - zinc-coated steel:
                      - uncoated: *Iron*

Covering   - of copper or metal:
                      - zinc: *Teakwood skin and zinc*

Indicate where the ship was surveyed, and whether according to the full or abbreviated procedure of the Ship Survey Regulation of 5 July 1872, and with submission of the earlier ship survey certificate.

Hamburg
Net 199,9 cubic metre - 70,56 British tons

Name of builder, year of construction, place of construction. The following documents must be submitted: deletion from the registry of the earlier home port, time and construction, if applicable, the earlier name of the ship, and for foreign ships, indicate the circumstances under which the ship obtained the right to fly a German flag, or is applying for that right.

Built in 1865 at Hevne near Christiansund

New home port: *Hamburg*

Agreed
J. A. Jacobsen

Page 2 of 11

Name, designation and location of the domicile of the owners, indicating the size of the share in the ship of each partial owner.

Carl Gottfried Wilhelm Heinrich Hagenbeck, land-based owner in Hamburg
1/3 share

and

Jacob Martin Jacobsen in Hamburg
2/3 share

Page 3 of 11

Legal reason on which is based the acquisition of the property in each share (Bill of Sale of, if available 'Bielbrief' [transfer certificate], have to be submitted.

Bill of sale dated Kristiansund the 8th of December 1879

Name and location of residence of the Captain:

Number of regular crew including the Captain: 8
(For steamers, indicate the engineer(s))

Number of ship's chronometers: 1

I or we promise herewith to notify the authorities as soon as possible if any changes occur.

Hamburg,

Carl Hagenbeck
J. Martin Jacobsen

Page 4 of 11

Carl Hagenbeck's Thierpark   Hamburg, ... 18...
13 Neuer Pferdemakt

Carl Gottfried Wilhelm Heinrich Hagenbeck
ship's owner with 1/3 share in the galeas Eisbär

Jacob Martin Jacobsen with 2/3 shares in the galeas Eisbär

Page 5 of 11

Deputation for trade and shipping

The following local citizens appeared here:

Carl Gottfried Wilhelm Heinrich Hagenbeck and
Jakob Martin Jakobsen and
Johann Adrian Jakobsen

and they stated the following:

The ownership of the Galeas Hevegutten now named Eisbär had changed as follows, and that according to a 'bill of sale' dated at Kristiansund the 8th of December 1879, the above-mentioned gentlemen stated that the shared ownership in the ship has changed to sole ownership of C. Hagenbeck and of J. M. Jacobsen, that is to say the first mentioned 1/3 share, and the latter 2/3 share.

Hamburg, 9 April 1880
Carl Hagenbeck
J. Martin Jacobsen

Agreed
J. A. Jacobsen

Recorded:
Meinke
Ship surveyor

Carl Gottfried Wilhelm Heinrich Hagenbeck
ship's owner with 1/3 share in the galeas Eisbär

Jacob Martin Jacobsen with 2/3 shares in the galeas Eisbär

Page 6 of 11

Ship Survey Certificate

The undersigned authority hereby certifies that the sailing ship named *Eisbär*, with the recognition signal *RFVM* under the *German* flag and home port *Hamburg* commanded by the skipper [left blank] was surveyed according to the Ship Survey Regulation of 5 July 1872 according to the complete procedure.

The ship was built at *Christiansund* in the year 1865. The principal building material is *wood*. Below the deck used for the survey there is *no other* deck. On the uppermost deck there *is an* addition. The shape of the deck is *flat*. The outer part of the hull *is clad in zinc* [plated steel]. The ship has *two* masts and is rigged as a *schooner* [galeas].

The total length of the ship is *23.15 m*
The greatest width of the ship is...
The height of the cargo space between the uppermost surface of the solid deck and the upper edge of the inboard [inner?] covering beside the wheel, the diameter is *2,88 m*

Page 7 of 11

The size of the cargo volume measures as follows:

	m^3	British tons
Space below the deck	204,2	72,00
Space between the decks		
Space above the surveyed deck and addition	6,2	2,19
The gross tonnage of the ship is thus	210,4	74,27
Subtracted from this is the space allocated to the crew members who are *located in the front*,	10,5	3,71

below the deck within the addition, 1/20 of the total
surveyed volume:
The net cargo volume of the ship   199,9   70,56

Hamburg, 8 April 1880

The Revision Authority ship surveys
OW Oswald

Page 8 of 11

[Handwritten letter from the Swedish or Norwegian? Consulate General in Hamburg. Signed by Munch Reider. Has not been translated.]

Page 9 of 11

No 1136
Hamburg, the 28th of June 1883

To the Office of Trade and Shipping

I hereby transfer to you the ownership of the ship Eisbär because I have sold the ship at Hammerfest.

J. Martin Jacobsen

Page 10 of 11

[Ship's certificate dated April 9, 1880. Contains the same information as the certificates on pages 6 & 7. A black line has been drawn on it from top left to bottom right corner and the mention 'certificate cancelled on July 9, 1883,' was added in top-right corner.]

Page 11 of 11

[Back of the ship's certificate with the information about the two shareholders (same information as found on page 4.)

Decreased demand and value of German sailing vessels like the *Eisbär* in 1883

By Dieter Riedel, M.Sc, Ph.D.

According to *Fischfang und Fischwirtschaft* [Fishery and Fishery Economics] (Institut für Geographie. Universität Stuttgart. n.d.), by 1880, in North German harbour cities like Hamburg, there was a demand mostly for steam powered ships larger than the sailing ship *Eisbär*, and therefore the use and value of these kinds of sailing ships decreased. The underlying reason for this was the growth of cities through development of railway networks. In the 1870s, the railways connected large harbour cities to large industrial cities in the interior. The growth of the cities inside Germany increased the demand for herring and for other marine fish, and the railways could quickly bring large amounts of both salted or pickled fish, or freshly caught fish which was kept on ice, from the North Sea or Baltic coasts to inland cities.

In response to the increased demand for marine fish, steam-powered ships of several hundred tons began to replace the sail-powered and generally slower and smaller fishing vessels for fishing beyond the North Sea. This trend from sail to steam was especially pronounced in Hamburg, whose main economic activity was international trade with large vessels, rather than coastal or North Sea fishing with small vessels. Moreover, much of Hamburg's trade was with Denmark, Norway, and Great Britain, and from them it imported large amounts of fish (Baartz 1991). Therefore, by 1880, the owners of fishery sailing ships like the *Eisbär* had to compete both with larger steam powered ships, and with imported fish. As a result, by 1883, galeases like the *Eisbär* were no longer in as much demand as when they had been built.

Afterword

Johan Adrian Jacobsen's archive and collections in the *Museum am Rothenbaum*, Hamburg
By Christine Chávez and Barbara Plankensteiner[1]

It is our pleasure to add some afterthoughts to this publication and endeavour that draw heavily from documents preserved in the *Museum am Rothenbaum* (MARKK). The book contributes to making archival records available to a large interested readership, and particularly to descendants of individuals and communities who once interacted with Jacobsen or participated in the human shows that he organized. Only the translation into English provides better access to these historical records.

We increasingly experience that writings of the late 19th and early 20th century German travelers, researchers or colonialists who wrote down their experiences are of special interest to those people whose forebears had once been studied or visited during the colonial period. We see it as one of our major obligations to increase the accessibility of the archival records in our holdings. There is still a long way to go to digitize not only those, but also the museum's photographs and object collections and to make them available online.

Our photograph and document archives also play a central role in in the museum's repositioning process which has started in 2017 and entailed the museum's recent name change[2] and revision of its mission, displays, and programs. The archives enable us to better understand the historical context of the formation and function of our object collections in a way that is different from how they were seen in the past. We now put an emphasis on provenance research, looking for traces of individual ownership of objects and seeking to reconstruct the identity of individuals whose names were not recorded with the photographs in which they were portrayed.

Among the many photographic and document archives that the museum houses today, Johan Adrian Jacobsen's archive has always held a prominent place. Long before his archive and object collection found their way into the then *Museum für Völkerkunde Hamburg*, they were first assembled and exhibited in November 1933 in a special 'Jacobsen room' in the old town hall of the then independent city of Altona.[3] Prior to this date, Jacobsen had donated them to the German Nordic Society of Hamburg, but they had remained in his house in Stellingen-Altona until Paul Theodor Hoffmann, head of the City Archive of Altona, contacted Jacobsen in May 1933 and convinced him to transfer them to the City Archive.

It had been Jacobsen's strong wish to preserve his archive and collection and to make them accessible for his children and the public, something he obviously felt the City Archive would be in a better position to guarantee. In order to avoid trouble, Jacobsen's donation to the German Nordic Society remained valid. Yet in the custody of the City Archive, with the condition that nothing should be sold, and in event the Nordic Society no longer existed, the archive and the collection would become the city's property.

During the fall of 1933, boxes and lockers containing his small ethnographical collection, library, photographs, diaries, written records, letters, newspaper cuttings, and other documents were all moved to the town hall to be stored and exhibited there. It seems, however, that accessibility and the presentation of the archive was not maintained at the intended level. At any rate, inadequate accessibility was Franz Termer's argument when he, as newly appointed director of the *Museum für Völkerkunde Hamburg* since 1935, made his first attempt to relocate Jacobsen's donation from Altona to the ethnological museum in June 1936. Despite Jacobsen's approval for these plans, the attempt failed, because the archive belonged to the city of Altona and, therefore, to the Prussian State. Yet, things changed rather quickly.

In 1938, Altona became part of the Free City of Hamburg, and in the summer of 1940 the City Archive of Altona handed over the complete archive to the ethnological museum. In April 1941, the museum held a small event in Jacobsen's honor. Even during war time, after Jacobsen had moved to Risøya in Norway, he was concerned about the whereabouts of his archive. In 1944, he asked if it was still intact. After the war, efforts were made to reorder the archive and several photographs and documents that were deemed irrelevant to the museum were handed over to Hagenbeck's archive and to the *Museum für Hamburgische Geschichte* in 1948.

Today, the *Museum am Rothenbaum* houses the relatively small ethnographic collection[4] from the City Archive Altona with artefacts from Norway, Germany, North America, Sri Lanka, and Indonesia of which about one third is missing and was probably destroyed during World War II. Apart from that, the museum also owns a Greenlandic collection[5] Jacobsen had assembled for Hagenbeck's ethnic show in 1877, which Carl Hagenbeck donated in 1878, and a few other objects that entered the museum via different persons or institutions. Although the Greenlandic collection is of interest due to its originating context, the size and quality of these object collections cannot be compared with Jacobsen's famous commissioned collections housed by other institutions.

In this regard, Jacobsen's photographic collection is of far higher relevance. It contains more than 1 680 photographs[6] taken by him and other individuals, predominantly in Europe and the Americas. Many of these images were taken during his voyages to recruit people for Hagenbeck's ethnic shows and offer glimpses into the circumstances of these enterprises.

Although there is mention of a library when transferring the Jacobsen archive to the museum in 1940, it was never really mentioned again after World War II. For now, it remains unclear whether this library was actually taken over and if or how it was incorporated into the museum's inventory.

The document archive finally makes up for the largest part of Jacobsen's collections. Together with the photographic collection, it constitutes an invaluable archive for infinite research questions regarding Jacobsen's legacy. During a pilot project from 2011 to 2014, all documents were packed according to archival standards and partly digitized to make them accessible for scientific research and other external visitors. Today, they are stored in 58 archival boxes comprising his diaries, vast correspondence from 1871 until 1939, graphical documents, maps, plans and bills, newspaper clippings, reports on his journeys, lists, lectures, articles, and so forth.

The number of research requests on Jacobsen's archive is constantly increasing. With provenance research representing one of the pressing needs of today's museum work and Johan Adrian Jacobsen's collections being scattered across many institutions, the Jacobsen archive clearly is of fundamental importance in shedding more light on the historic contexts and Jacobsen's own ambivalent and sometimes questionable role, as the case of Abraham Ulrikab and the other Labrador Inuit demonstrates.

Just as important is what we could learn about the many so far unheard voices and stories of individuals who crossed Jacobsen's path for better or for worse. Through Jacobsen's lens, there are many other histories to be found in his archive that can broaden our understanding of colonially shaped relationships. These histories are also essential for descendants of those individuals and their communities to know.

In this context, the research and translation work realized by France Rivet, Hartmut Lutz, Dieter Riedel and all others involved in this project is an outstanding example of how Jacobsen's archive can be fruitful for matters of the past, present and future.

---

[1] We are very grateful to Jantje Bruns (Library MARKK) and Cathi Winzer (Photographic Archive, MARKK) for providing us with the necessary archival material and a lot of useful information.

[2] The museum changed its name in September 2018 from *Museum für Völkerkunde Hamburg* to *Museum am Rothenbaum - World Cultures and Arts* (MARKK).

[3] The following paragraphs on the history of the Jacobsen archive refer to the museum's correspondence archived in file 101-1 Nr. 1303 (MARKK) and a few letters preserved in the Jacobsen archive (JAC 17.71, Nov 23, 1935 / JAC 17.71, Dec 12, 1935 / JAC 17.72, Jan 3, 1936).

[4] Catalogue numbers 40.34:1-34 and 40.35:1.

[5] Catalogue numbers B 1 to B 52.

[6] According to a count in 2005.

Archival Sources

MUSEUM AM ROTHENBAUM – KULTUREN AND KÜNSTE DER WELT, HAMBURG, GERMANY

Johan Adrian Jacobsen Archives, JAC.7.3.

BAUER, Edgar
 Letter to J. A. Jacobsen, Berlin, November 13, 1880.

HAGENBECK, Carl
 Letter to J. A. Jacobsen, Hamburg, November 9, 1880.
 Letter to J. A. Jacobsen, Hamburg, November 12, 1880.
 Letter to J. A. Jacobsen, Hamburg, December 26, 1880.

Johan Adrian Jacobsen Archives, JAC.7.4.

BAUER, Edgar
 Letter to J. A. Jacobsen, Berlin, November 13, 1880.
 Letter to J. A. Jacobsen, /Berlin?/, January 20, 1881
 Letter to J. A. Jacobsen, Berlin, February 5, 1881.
 Letter to J. A. Jacobsen, Düsseldorf, March 27, 1881.

BASTIAN, Adolf
 Letter to J. A. Jacobsen, Berlin, January 20, 1881.
 Letter to J. A. Jacobsen, Berlin, April 4, 1881.
 Letter to J. A. Jacobsen, Berlin, April 5, 1881.

HAGENBECK, Carl
    Letter to J. A. Jacobsen, Hamburg, January 16, 1881.
    Letter to J. A. Jacobsen, Hamburg, January 27, 1881.
    Letter to J. A. Jacobsen, Hamburg, Febuary 17, 1881.
    Letter to J. A. Jacobsen, Hamburg, September 23, 1881.
    Letter to J. A. Jacobsen, Hamburg, December 2, 1881.

JACOBSEN, Jacob Martin
    Letter to J. A. Jacobsen, [St. Pauli], January 17, 1881.
    Letter to J. A. Jacobsen, St. Pauli, January 27, 1881.

JACOBSEN, Johan Adrian
    List of Inuit objets and invoice for Prof. Bogisic, Paris, January 14, 1881.

KÜHNE, Carl Friedrich Ludwig
    Letter to J. A. Jacobsen, Altona, January 14, 1881.
    Letter to J. A. Jacobsen, Altona, February 7, 1881.

KÜHNE, Henriette (Henny)
    Letter to J. A. Jacobsen, St. Pauli, January 10, 1881.
    Letter to J. A. Jacobsen, [St. Pauli], January 13, 1881.
    Letter to J. A. Jacobsen, [St. Pauli], January 17, 1881.
    Letter to J. A. Jacobsen, St. Pauli, January 27, 1881.

LUTZ, Albertina
    Letter to J. A. Jacobsen, Munich, January 30, 1881.

SCHOEPF, Adolf
    Letter to J. A. Jacobsen, Paris, January 23, 1881.
    Letter to J. A. Jacobsen, Paris, January 24, 1881.
    Letter to J. A. Jacobsen, Paris, January 27, 1881.

Postcard to J. A. Jacobsen, Hamburg, February 15, 1881.
Letter to J. A. Jacobsen, Hamburg, February 17, 1881.
Postcard to J. A. Jacobsen, Hamburg, June 8, 1881.

Johan Adrian Jacobsen Archives, JAC.19.6.2

JACOBSEN, Johan Adrian
Ein Seemannsleben (Manuscript). pp. 61–66.

Johan Adrian Jacobsen Archives, 2011.37.1.

JACOBSEN, Johan Adrian
Tagebuch ('Journal'). pp. 78–158.

STAATSARCHIV HAMBURG
HAMBURG, GERMANY

Galeasse *Eisbär*, Seeschiffsregisternummer 1136. Source: 231-4_1203. (11 pages)

NUNATTA KATERSUGAASIVIA ALLAGAATEQARFIALU (GREENLAND NATIONAL MUSEUM AND ARCHIVES) NUUK, GREENLAND

Letters from governor T. S. Krarup Smith in Godhavn to 1) Jacobsen and 2) Trade manager Møller with instructions about how to handle Jacobsens requests (Governors Archive - Letter journal - NKA 0102/11.12/25)

Letters from governor T. S. Krarup Smith to Kongelige Grønlandske Handel in Copenhagen about Jacobsens arrival and visits. (Governors Archive - Letter journal - Breve til Direktionen - NKA 01.02/11.22/15)

RIGSARKIVET (DANISH NATIONAL ARCHIVES), COPENHAGEN, DENMARK

Direktoratet Kgl. Grønlandske Handel, Indkomne breve 1880–18811, no 21,

JACOBSEN, Johan Adrian
 Letter to the North Greenland Inspector, Jakobshavn, July 7, 1880. Page 4 of 6.
 Letter to the North Greenland Inspector, Jakobshavn, July 20, 1880. Page 6 of 6.

KRARUP SMITH, Theodor
 Letter to J. A. Jacobsen, Godhavn, July 14, 1880. Page 5 of 6.

CULTURE AND SOCIAL SCIENCE LIBRARY THE ARCTIC UNIVERSITY OF NORWAY, TROMSØ, NORWAY

Finmarkspoften. No. 35. August 25, 1885.

Ishavfangsten fra hammerfest *in Norsk Fiskeritidende. kvartalsskrift udgivet af Selskabet for de norske Fiskeriers Fremme*. 1886. Bergen: Griegs Bogtrntteri. pp. 88-89.

REGIONAL STATE ARCHIVES TROMSØ, NORWAY

Tromsø Tollsted Vaktjournal - Indførede Ishavsprodukter for Aaret 1885, Statsarkivet, Tromsø.

Hammerfest Tollsted 1883 (Customs records)
Hammerfest Tollsted 1884 (Customs records)
Hammerfest Tollsted 1885 (Customs records)

NORWEGIAN POLAR INSTITUTE
TROMSØ, NORWAY

Vessel database - record for ship "Eisber"

Other References

Atalic, Bruno. 2016. *1885 Cholera Controversy: Klein versus Koch.* Accessed on October 1, 2018 at <http://citeseerx.ist.psu.edu/viewdoc/download?doi=10.1.1.825.1271&rep=rep1&type=pdf>

Baartz, Roland. 1991. Entwicklung und Strukturwandel der deutschen Hochseefischerei. In: *Mitteilungen der Geogr. Gesellschaft in Hamburg,* vol 81, 664 pp.

Behbehani, Abbas M. 1983. The Smallpox Story: Life and Death of an Old Disease. *Microbiology Reviews.* 47.4:455–509.

Brahm, Felix. 2005. Weise du schufest die Wehr, die Hamburgs Pockenschutz gründet, die Geschichte des Hamburger Impfzentrums von den Anfängen der Pockenimpfung bis zur Gegenwart, unter Mitarbeit von Tatjana Timoschenko. (In English: The history of the vaccination clinic of the Institute of Hygiene and Environment in Hamburg, from the beginning of vaccination to the present, with contributions of Tatjana Timoschenko.) In: *Schriftenreihe des Instituts für Hygiene und Umwelt,* Hamburg. Bremen:Ed. Temmen. 2:294-295.

Brueckner, Hedwig. 1987. *Translation of the diary kept by Captain Johan Adrian Jacobsen on Board the Galleas Eisbaer 1880,* unpublished.

St. John's: Memorial University Library (Center for Newfoundland Studies).

Chang, Huan J., Cassio, Lynm, and Glass, Richard M. 2009. JAMA Patient Page. Typhoid Fever. *JAMA*. 302.8:914. Accessed on October 1, 2018 at
<https://jamanetwork.com/journals/jama/fullarticle/184468>

Colin, Léon. 1881. L'épidémie de variole des Esquimaux et de la réceptivité spéciale des nouveaux venus dans les foyers épidémiques. *Bulletin de l'Académie nationale de médecine*. 2.X:356-371. Accessed on October 1, 2018 at
<http://gallica.bnf.fr/ark:/12148/bpt6k408671n>

Evans, Alfred S. 1973. Pettenkofer revisited. The life and contributions of Max von Pettenkofer 1818-1901. *Yale Journal of Biology and Medicine*. 46:161-176.

Institut für Geographie. Universität Stuttgart. n.d. *Fischfang und Fischwirtschaft*. 6-8. Accessed on June 28, 2018 at
<http://www.geographie.uni-stuttgart.de/exkursionsseiten/Nwd2001/Themen_pdf/Fischfang.pdf>

Jacobi, Carl R. E. 1875. *Das Reichs-Impf-Gesetz vom 8. April 1874; nebst Ausführungs-Bestimmungen des Bundesraths und den in Geltung gebliebenen Landes-Gesetzen u¨ber Zwangs-Impfungen bei Pocken-Epidemien*. (In English: The Imperial vaccination law of April 8th, 1874, with an Implementation regulations of the Federal Council and the different still valid national laws on obligatory vaccinations during smallpox epidemics.) Berlin: Fr. Kortkampf, Publisher of Imperial Laws. 94 pp.

Jacobsen, Johan Adrian. 1894. *Eventyrlige Farter, Fortalte for Ungdommen*. Bergen: John Griegs Forlag. Translation by Ingeborg v.d Lippe Konow. 43–50. Accessed at the National Library of Norway (Oslo)

Jacobsen, Johan Adrian. 1912. *Aus den Jugendjahren meines Seemanslebens*. Deutsche Jugendbücherei Nr. 73. Berlin-Leipzig: Hermann Hillger. 32 pp.

Jacobsen, Johan Adrian. 1931. *Die weisse Grenze: Abenteuer eines alten Seebaren rund um den Polarkreis* [The White Frontier: Adventures of an Old Sailor All Around the Arctic Circle]. Leipzig: F.A. Brockhaus.

Leavitt, J.W. 1996. *Typhoid Mary. Captive to the public's health*. Boston: Beacon Press. 335 pp.

Lutz, Hartmut, Alootook Ipellie, Hans-Ludwig Blohm. (2005). *The Diary of Abraham Ulrikab: Text and Context*. Ottawa: University of Ottawa Press. xxvii, 100 p.

Ogawa, Mariko. 2000. Uneasy bedfellows: Science and politics in the refutation of Koch's bacterial theory of cholera. *Bulletin of the History of Medicine*. 74:671-707.

Rivet, France. 2014. *In the Footsteps of Abraham Ulrikab: The Events of 1880–1881*. Gatineau: Polar Horizons.

Sefton, A. M. 2008. The Great Pox that was…syphilis. *Journal of Applied Microbiology*. 91.4:592-596. Accessed on October 1, 2018 at <https://onlinelibrary.wiley.com/doi/full/10.1046/j.1365-2672.2001.01494.x>

The Free Dictionary. 2018. *Ex Post Facto Laws*. Accessed on October 1, 2018 at <https://legal-dictionary.thefreedictionary.com/Ex+Post+Facto+Laws.>

Wikipedia. 2018a. *Koch-Pasteur Rivalry*. Accessed on October 1, 2018 at <https://en.wikipedia.org/wiki/Koch%E2%80%93Pasteur_rivalry>

Wikipedia. 2018b. *Mary Mallon*. Accessed on October 1, 2018 at <https://en.wikipedia.org/wiki/Mary_Mallon>

Wikipedia. 2018c. *Ex post facto law*. Accessed on October 1, 2018 at <https://en.wikipedia.org/wiki/Ex_post_facto_law>

Wikipedia. 2018d. *German Gold Mark*. Accessed on October 1, 2018 at <https://en.wikipedia.org/wiki/German_gold_mark>

Index of People and Place Names

Folios in italics refer to end of chapter notes. Those in bold refer to illustrations and their captions.

A

Aachen, **165**
    mentions in J. A. Jacobsen's diary, 166, 174, 176, 179, 186
    mentions in letters from Adolf Schoepf, 236, 237, 238, 239, 253
    mentions in letters from C. L. Kühne, 249
    mentions in letters from Carl Hagenbeck, 240, 254
    mentions in letters from Edgar Bauer, 247
Abraham. *See* Ulrikab, Abraham
Abyssinia, 188
Aix-la-Chapelle. *See* Aachen
Akunnat. *See* Lichtenfels
Alaska, 177
Albert Edward (Prince of Wales), 185, *196*
Altona, 189, 278, 279
    letters written in, 226, 249
Amundsen, Roald, **42**
Ane, 88, **92**, *94*, *Also see* Greenlanders (the group of 1877)
Angmagssalik, 73
Arsuit, 136

B

Baffin Island. *See* Baffinland
Baffinland, 62, 82, 83

Baglo, Cathrine, 34, **35**, 41, *58*, *196*
Bang (Captain), 53, 57, 69, 70, 76, 91, 99, 103, 112, 125
Barton Holiman, Kirsten Katharina, 38, 39, 41, **43**
Bastian, Adolf
    letters to J. A. Jacobsen, 235, 258, 259
    mentions of him in J. A. Jacobsen's diary, 176, 177, 186, 190
    mentions of him in letters from Adolf Schoepf, 238
    mentions of him in letters from Edgar Bauer, 218, 234, 247, 256
Bauer, Edgar
    letters to J. A. Jacobsen, 234, 247, 256
    mentions of him in letters from Adolf Bastian, 235, 259
    mentions of him in letters from Adolf Schoepf, 238
Bedranowsky, Kerstin, 39, **40**
Bergen, 51, 91, 207
Berlin, **144**
    letters written in, 218, 234, 235, 247, 258, 259
    mentions in J. A. Jacobsen's diary, 57, 145, 146, 150, 151, 153, 176, 177, 184, 185, 186, 189, 190, 191
    mentions in letters from Adolf Schoepf, 238
    mentions in letters from Carl Hagenbeck, 260, 262

Blohm, Hans-Ludwig, 21, **22**, **27**
Bockum, **160**, 162
Bogišić, Valtazar, 223, 224, 225
Brahm, Felix, 193, 195
Bremen, 189, 242
Bremenhaven, 241, 253
Breslau, 184, 186
British Columbia, 17, 177, 190
Brun, Carsten, 68, 70
Bruns, Jantje, **26**
Brunshausen, 61, *84*
Budapest, 253
Busch, 145

C

Cape Walers, *105*
Capetown. *See* Good Hope, Cape of
Cécile (Sister), 170, 171, 172
Chile, 176
Christensen (sailor), 58
Christiania, 70
Christianssund, 51, 52, 53, 268, 272, *See also* Kristiansund
Coleman, Arthur Philemon, **105**, **107**, **109**, **123**, **200**
Copenhagen, 88, 91, 213
Crefeld, **144**, 157, 158, 159, **163**, 176
Cumberland Sound, **60**, 80, 81, 82, 83, 93, *105*, 199, 211, 214
Cuxhaven, 56, 61, 145, 146, 147, 180

D

Darmstadt, **144**, 157, 161
Davis Strait, **60**, 70, 74, 75, 79, 80, 83, 94, 132
Disko Bay, **60**, 83, 84
Disko Island, 84
Dog Island, 96
Dogger Bank, 55
Dotto, Baptist, 177
Dresden, 124, 150, 190
Düsseldorf, 179, 259
  letters written in, 256

E

East India, 181

Easter Islands, 176
Elsner, Augustus Ferdinand, 189, *196*
Elson, George, *118*, *119*
Emsbüttel, 183
Ericsson, Leif, 115
Erquelinnes, 165
Ethiopia, 188

F

Fair Isle, 136
Falke (ship pilot), 52
Farewell, Cape, **60**, 75, 76, 77, *118*, 134
Faroe Islands, 64, 65, 75, 80, 137, **144**
Felsberg, Susan, *130*
Fjordane, 51
Fleischer, Carl, 87, 125
Fleischer, Knud Geelmuyden, 91
Föhr, 141
Ford, George, 116, 122, **123**, 124, 125
Foula, *139*
Francke, E.C., 177
Frankfurt, **144**, 154, 155
Friedrichsthal, 108, *118*
Frobisher Bay, 82, 84

G

Geneva, 243
Gismerøya, *56*
Glückstadt, 51, *54*, 145
Godhavn, **60**, 84, 88, 90, 91, 92, 96, 214
  letters written in, 212
Goldberger, Ludwig M., 177
Good Hope, Cape of, 183
Gravesend, 181
Gray, Alexander, 122, 124, *130*
Greenland, 17, **60**
  mentions in J. A. Jacobsen's diary, 62, 73, 78, 81, 83, 87, 89, 108, 109, 110, 113, 114, 115, 125, 131, 136
  mentions in J. A. Jacobsen's letters, 214, 215, 218, 224, 225
  mentions in letters from Edgar Bauer, 234

Greenlanders (the group of 1877), 19,
Also See Ana, Kokkik, Kujanje,
Magak, Okabak, Regine
   mentions of them in J. A. Jacobsen's
diary, 87, 89, 93, 108, 146, 149,
166
   mentions of them in letters from
Carl Hagenbeck, 262
   mentions of them in letters from
Krarup Smith, 212
Gulliksen (sailor), 57, *58*

H

Hagenbeck, Carl, 15, 16, 17, **29**, 31, **33**,
85, *94*, **178**, 195, 233, 279
   Eisbär ship registration, 269, 270,
271
   letters to J. A. Jacobsen, 216, 217,
219, 228, 240, 254, 260, 262
   mentions of him in J. A. Jacobsen's
diary, 51, 52, 114, 145, 146, 147,
149, 158, 159, 166, 173, 175, 177,
179, 180, 181, 183, 187, 188, 189,
190, 191
   mentions of him in letters from
Adolf Schoepf, 236, 243, 255
   mentions of him in letters from C. L.
Kühne, 250
   mentions of him in letters from
Edgar Bauer, 234, 256
   mentions of him in letters from
Henriette Kühne, 231, 241, 242,
251, 252
   mentions of him in letters from
Jacob Martin Jacobsen, 229, 230,
242
Hagenbeck, Claus Gottfried Carl, 145
Hagenbeck, John, 180, 181, 183
Hamburg, 25, 27, 29, 33, 38, 39, **59**,
144, **184**, 191, 192, 195, 275
   Eisbär ship registration, 268, 269,
270, 271, 272, 273
   letters written in, 216, 217, 219,
228, 229, 240, 253, 254, 255, 260,
262
   mentions in J. A. Jacobsen's diary,
51, 53, 56, 61, 70, 133, 137, 138,
145, 146, 147, 149, 166, 174, 175,
176, 177, 179, 180, 183, 184, 186,
188, 189, 190
   mentions in letters from Adolf
Bastian, 258
   mentions in letters from Adolf
Schoepf, 237, 238, 253
Hammerfest, 34, 35, 36, *44*, 273
Hansen, Johann, 251
Haugk, W., 107
Hawaii, 177
Hebron, *18*, 19, **20**, **60**, 104, **107**, 108,
111, 117, 124, 128, **129**, *130*, 132,
134
Hecker, Emil, 177
Heligoland, 56, 62, 141, **143**, **144**, 188
Henny. *See* Kühne, Henriette (Henny)
Hevne, 33, 52, 267, 268
Hoffmann, M., **88**, **111**, **141**, 149
Hoffmann, Paul Theodor, 278
Hopedale, 108
Horsten (Family), 251
Hörten, 242
Hubbard, Leonidas, *118*, *119*
Hubbard, Mina, *119*
Hudson Strait, 84

I

Iceland, 51, 68, 80, 135, 136, 242
Ilulissat. *See* Jakobshavn
Ingstad, Helge, *119*
Iqaluit. *See* Frobisher Bay

J

Jacobi (Dr.), 160, 162
Jacobi, Carl, 194
Jacobs (Mrs.), 149, *151*, 157, 161, 163,
175, 179, 238
Jacobsen, Adrian, 39, **40**
Jacobsen, Anne Kirsti, **13**
Jacobsen, Hans, 35
Jacobsen, Jacob Martin, **33**, 34, *84*,
126, **129**, 232, 233
   Eisbär ship registration, 269, 270,
271, 273
   letters to J. A. Jacobsen, 229, 242

mentions of him in J. A. Jacobsen's
diary, 51, 52, 61, 145, 146, 177,
190
mentions of him in letters from
Adolf Schoepf, 253
mentions of him in letters from C. L.
Kühne, 227, 249, 250
mentions of him in letters from
Henriette Kühne, 241, 251, 252
Jacobsen, Johan Adrian, **13**, 15, 17, 19,
20, 21, 23, 27, 28, 31, **33**, 35, 36, **38**,
42, 45, 192, 195, 278, 279, 280
Eisbär ship registration, 269, 270,
271
letters written by him, 211, 214, 224
Jakobshavn, 16, 36, **60**, **90**, **92**, **94**, 212
letters written in, 211, 214
mentions in J. A. Jacobsen's diary,
83, 87, 88, 96, 99
Jamrach, Charles, 188, *196*
Jamrach, William, 187, 188, *196*
Jan Mayen, 70, 71
Jensen, Johannes Hendrik. See Kujanje
Johanne Juditte Margrethe. See
Maggak
Josephsson, Helena, 246
Junker (Möller's assistant), 96

K

Kamchatka, 177
Kangerdluksoak. *See* Hebron
Kangiqsujuaq, *105*
Kaufmann (Mr.), 188
Kitsissuarsuit. *See* Dog Island
Klein, Emanuel Edward, 192
Kleven, 55, 56
Knudsen (Möller's assistant), 96
Koch, Robert, 192
Kokkik, 88, **92**, *94*, *Also see*
Greenlanders (the group of 1877)
Koppmann, Georg, **59**
Krabbe, Thomas Neergaard, **90**
Krarup Smith, Theodore, 36, 81, 83, 88,
92
letters to J. A. Jacobsen, 212
Krefeld. *See* Crefeld
Krell, E., **162**
Kretschmer, Carl Gottlieb, 107, *118*

Kreuzberg (Mr.), 243
Kristiansund, 33, 34, 58, **144**, 269, 271,
Also see Christianssund
Kronegh, Adam Jon, 37
Kühne, Carl Friedrich Ludwig
letters to J. A. Jacobsen, 226, 249
Kühne, Henriette (Henny), *84*, 232, 233
letters to J. A. Jacobsen, 220, 222,
231, 241, 251
mentions of her in J. A. Jacobsen's
diary, 61
mentions of her in letters from C. L.
Kühne, 226, 249
Kujanje, 16, 88, **92**, *94*, *Also see*
Greenlanders (the group of 1877)
Kuril Islands, 177, *178*

L

L'Anse aux Meadows, *119*
Labrador, 17, **60**, 83, **109**
mentions in J. A. Jacobsen's diary,
77, 89, 103, 104, 109, 113, 114,
131, 176
mentions in J. A. Jacobsen's letters,
218, 234
Labrador Inuit (the group of), 23, 24,
28, 39, 192, 194, 195, 233, *Also see*
Ulrikab, Abraham; Ulrike; Tobias;
Tigianniak; Paingu, Nuggasak; Sara;
Maria
mentions of them in J. A. Jacobsen's
diary, 52, 128, 131, 133, 134, 137,
142, 145, 146, 147, 149, 151, 153,
154, 157, 159, 165, 166, 167, 168,
189, 191
mentions of them in letters from
Adolf Bastian, 235, 258
mentions of them in letters from
Adolf Schoepf, 238, 244
mentions of them in letters from
Albertina Lutz, 245
mentions of them in letters from C.
L. Kühne, 226, 227
mentions of them in letters from
Carl Hagenbeck, 216, 217
mentions of them in letters from
Edgar Bauer, 247, 248

mentions of them in letters from
  Henriette Kühne, 220, 231, 252
mentions of them in letters from
  Jacob Martin Jacobsen, 230
mentions of them in letters from
  Mr. Martinet, 237
Lampe (sailor), 137, 138
Lampe, Johannes, 24, 27, **28**, 39, **40**
Landrin, Armand, 236, 238, 239, 243
Larsen Riedel, Doreen, 30
Leopold Island, 103, *105*
Lichtenfels, 108, *118*
Liebscher, Adolf, **150**, **151**, **154**, **155**, **158**, **168**, **169**, **174**
London, 117, 180, 181, **182**, 183, 187, 188, *196*
Lossius, Saras Michael Ideus, 34
Lough, Dave, 24
Ludwig (Pastor), 189
Lutz, Albertina, 245, 246
Lutz, Hartmut, 21, 22, 23, 25, **26**, **27**, **28**, **29**, 31, 41, **43**, 199, 281
Lyngen, 56

M

Magellan, Strait of, 176
Maggak, 88, 92, *94*, *Also see* Greenlanders (the group of 1877)
Mainz, 159
Mandal, 55, *56*
Mannheim, 177
Maria, **129**, **168**, *Also see* Labrador Inuit (the group of)
  mentions of her in J. A. Jacobsen's diary, 128, 167, 168
Martinet (Mr.), 175, 236, 239
  letters to J. A. Jacobsen, 237
Maurer, Wilhelm, 177
Melanesia, 177
Micronesia, 177
Mikalsen, Kenth Thomas, 38, **42**
Möller, Ernst Viggo, 87, 89, 91, *94*, 96
Mongeau, Diane, **60**, **144**
Müller-Küchler, Carl, 161
Munich, 154
  letters written in, 245

N

Nachvak, 21, **60**, 116, 117, 118, *119*, 121, **123**, **126**, 128, **132**, 199, **200**
Nain, 108
Namur, 165
Nansen, Fridtjof, **42**, 251
Narsarmijit. *See* Friedrichsthal
New York, 82
Newfoundland, 113, 114, 115, 118, *119*
Noahssen, Hans. *See* Kokkik
Nochasak, Zipporah, 21
Norway, 17, 89, 205, 207, 233
Nøtterøy, *58*
Novaya Zemlya, 80
Nuggasak, 21, 46, **126**, **155**, **158**, **162**, *Also see* Labrador Inuit (the group of)
  mentions of her in J. A. Jacobsen's diary, 121, 125, 128, 133, 134, 157, 160, 161, 166

O

Okabak, 88, **92**, 93, *94*, 211, *Also see* Greenlanders (the group of 1877)
Okak, 108
Oqaatsut. *See* Rodebay, *See* Rodebay
Oslo. *See* Christiania
Oswald, O.W., 273

P

Paingu, 16, 22, 46, **126**, **151**, **155**, **162**, *Also see* Labrador Inuit (the group of)
  mentions of her in J. A. Jacobsen's diary, 121, 125, 128, 142, 157, 158, 160, 161, 166, 176
  mentions of her in letters from C. L. Kühne, 226
  mentions of her in letters from Carl Hagenbeck, 216, 219
Pálfy (Mr.), 187, 188, 189
Panneval (Dr.), 29, **30**
Paris, 21, 23, 24, 29, **144**, *170*
  letters written in, 224, 236, 238, 243
  mentions in J. A. Jacobsen's diary, 110, 166, 170, 172, 175, 176

mentions in letters from Adolf
  Bastian, 258
mentions in letters from Adolf
  Schoepf, 237, 253
mentions in letters from C. L. Kühne,
  249
mentions in letters from Carl
  Hagenbeck, 228, 260, 262, 263
mentions in letters from Henriette
  Kühne, 220, 223, 231
Pasteur, Louis, 192
Patagonia, 176
Patagonians (the group of 1881)
  mentions of them in J. A. Jacobsen's
    diary, 52
  mentions of them in letters from
    Adolf Schoepf, 236
  mentions of them in letters from
    Carl Hagenbeck, 260, 262, 263
  mentions of them in letters from
    Henriette Kühne, 241
Pechler (zoo keeper), 185
Pelletier, Gilles, 29
Polynesia, 176, 177
Poulsen, Mikkel Kaspar Zacharias. *See*
  Okabak
Prague, 111, **144**, 153, 154, 159, 245
Prince of Wales, Cape, *105*
Punto Arenas, 176

Q

Qeqertarsuaq. *See* Godhavn
Queen Charlotte Islands, 177

R

Ramah, 107, 108, 117
Rasmussen, Christian Vilhelm, 91, *94*
Rasmussen, Knud, 91
Regine, 88, **92**, *94*, Also see
  Greenlanders (the group of 1877)
Reider, Munch, 273
Reiherstieg, 184
Reimers, Johan, 95
Reiss, Carl, 177
Richter, Isidor, 177
Riedel, Dieter, 30, **31**, 34, 191, 205,
  232, 275, 281

Risøya, 17, 24, 38, **41**, **42**, **43**, 279
Ritenbenk, 88, 90
Rivet, France, **20**, **22**, **26**, **27**, **28**, **29**, **31**,
  35, **38**, **40**, **41**, **42**, **43**, **132**, **170**, 281
Rodebay, 95, *96*
Rotterdam, 180

S

Saint-Hilaire, Geoffroy, 236
Saint-Quentin, 165
Sakhalin, 177
San Francisco, 260
Sara, **129**, **151**, Also see Labrador Inuit
  (the group of)
  mentions of her in J. A. Jacobsen's
    diary, 128, 160, 161, 163, 166
Saxony, 108
Schleswig, 141
Schneider, Johann Georg, 107
Schoepf, Adolf
  letters to J. A. Jacobsen, 236, 238,
    243, 253, 255
  mentions of him in J. A. Jacobsen's
    diary, 150, 157, 158, 159, 163,
    166, 167, 175, 190
  mentions of him in letters from
    Adolf Bastian, 258, 259
  mentions of him in letters from Carl
    Hagenbeck, 216, 219, 228, 240,
    254
Schoepf, Albin, 190
Schubert, Philip, *118*, *119*
Schwandorf, 154
Schweers (Captain), 180, 260
Scotland, 135, 136
Seiding, Inge, 36
Shetland Islands, 64, **144**
Skagerrak, 138, **144**
Smyth Channel, 176
South Africa, *196*
South America, 176, 180, 184
South Dakota, 17
Spitsbergen, 80, 89, 97
St. Pauli
  letters written in, 220, 222, 241
St. Petersburg, 145, 146
Stavanger, 51, *56*
Stechmann, Hermann, 159

Steiner (Mr.), 243
Stellingen, 39, 278
Stine, Anne, *119*
Stuberg, Joachim, 35, *44*
Sumburg Head, 138
Svalbard, 36
Sverdrup, Otto, **42**
Svinör, 55, *56*
Sweden, 17

T

Tasiilaq. *See* Angmagssalik
Termer, Franz, 279
Thun, Jacqueline, 25, **26**, 31
Tierra del Fuego, 176, *178*, 236
Tigianniak, 46, **126, 141, 150, 151, 155, 162, 169**, *Also see* Labrador Inuit (the group of)
  mentions of him in J. A. Jacobsen's diary, 121, 125, 128, 142, 143, 157, 158, 161, 167, 169
  mentions of him in J. A. Jacobsen's publications, 199, 203
Tobias, 23, 28, **129, 151, 154**, *Also see* Labrador Inuit (the group of)
  mentions of him in J. A. Jacobsen's diary, 128, 159, 162, 167, 169, 172, 173
Tønsberg, 53, 57, *58*
Tottingham, 183
Tromsø, 17, 34, 35, 37, 41, 52, 56, 242, 251, 252

U

Ulrikab, Abraham, 17, 19, 20, 21, 23, 24, 28, **129, 154, 174**, 196, 281, *Also see* Labrador Inuit (the group of)
  mentions of him in J. A. Jacobsen's diary, 116, 117, 118, 121, 124, 125, 128, 158, 159, 163, 167, 173
  mentions of him in letters from Edgar Bauer, 218
  mentions of him in letters from Jacob Martin Jacobsen, 229

Ulrike, 23, **129, 151, 168**, *Also see* Labrador Inuit (the group of)
  mentions of her in J. A. Jacobsen's diary, 128, 167, 173, 174, 175
  mentions of her in letters from Henriette Kühne, 231
  mentions of her in letters from Jacob Martin Jacobsen, 229
Umlauff, Johann Friedrich Gustav, 70, *85*
Ungava Bay, 124
Ungava Peninsula, *105*
Utsira, 55, *56*

V

Valdivia, 176
Vancouver Island, 177
Vienna, 236, 253
Virchow, Rudolf, 151, 186
Voigt, Leonhard, 195
von Bleichröder, G., 177
von der Lippe, Ingeborg, 143
von Haven, Lambert Christian, 87, 90, 94, 96
von LeCoq, August Albert, 177, 186, 187, 190
von Pettenkofer, Max Joseph, 192

W

Wadsö, 79, *85*
Walers, Cape, 103
Wallace, Dillon, *118*, *119*
Walter (Mr.), 158
Watchman Island, 104, 131
Weisbach, Valentin, 177
West Indies, 184
Wilhelm I (Emperor), 146
Wroclaw. *See* Breslau

Z

Zimmermann (Dr.), 162
Zoar, 108

OTHER TITLES PUBLISHED BY POLAR HORIZONS

IN THE FOOTSTEPS OF ABRAHAM ULRIKAB

In August 1880, two Labrador Inuit families were lured into becoming the latest attraction in European ethnographical shows. One participant, Abraham, was literate and keeping notes. Sadly, none of the eight individuals returned to their homeland. All died from smallpox while in Europe. More than 130 years after their death, *In the Footsteps of Abraham Ulrikab* tells the whole story, reveals the fate of their remains, and brings to light an opportunity for the Inuit's expressed wish to return to Labrador to eventually become a reality.

344 pages, 100 illustrations/photographs
ISBN 978-0-9936740-6-8 (softcover), 978-0-9936740-3-7 (PDF), 978-0-9936740-8-2 (epub)

RENATUS' KAYAK: A LABRADOR INUK, AN AMERICAN G.I. AND A SECRET WORLD WAR II WEATHER STATION

Renatus' Kayak is a true detective story that delves into military history, Inuit culture, wartime politics and a star-crossed love. The book's origin lies with a model sealskin kayak made in 1944 by Renatus Tuglavina and given to Woody Belsheim, a radio operator at the secret American weather station in Hebron, Labrador. Knowledge of the weather station and Renatus' life were lost to time until author Rozanne Enerson Junker, Woody's niece, began her quest, seventy years later.

215 pages, 69 photographs/illustrations
ISBN 978-1-7750815-0-0 (softcover)
ISBN 978-1-7750815-1-7 (epub)

www.ingramcontent.com/pod-product-compliance
Lightning Source LLC
Chambersburg PA
CBHW071806080526
44589CB00012B/703